ENGLISH LANGUAGE ARTS

English Language Arts offers both undergraduates and starting-graduate students in education an introduction to the connections that exist between language arts and a critical orientation to education. Because language influences all aspects of education, English teachers have a unique responsibility to create opportunities for learners to cultivate literacy practices that will empower them to reach their potential. Applying critical and theoretical perspectives to teaching English language arts, this primer considers how meanings are made in intersecting spaces of learners, teachers, and texts.

Julie Gorlewski shows future and current teachers how critical English language arts education can be put into practice with concrete strategies and examples in both formal and informal educational settings. With opportunities for readers to engage in deeper discussion through suggested activities, *English Language Arts'* pedagogical features include:

- Model Classroom Scenarios
- Extension Questions
- Glossary of Key Terms

Julie Gorlewski is associate professor and chair of the Department of Learning and Instruction at the University at Buffalo, The State University of New York. A former English teacher and editor of *English Journal*, she has published nine books and numerous articles and book chapters.

CRITICAL INTRODUCTIONS IN EDUCATION

Series Editor: Kenneth J. Saltman

For more information about this series, please visit: https://www.routledge.com/ Critical-Introductions-in-Education/book-series/CRITEDU

ENGLISH LANGUAGE ARTS

A Critical Introduction

Julie Gorlewski

Routledge
Taylor & Francis Group

NEW YORK AND LONDON

First published 2018
by Routledge
711 Third Avenue, New York, NY 10017

and by Routledge
2 Park Square, Milton Park, Abingdon, Oxon OX14 4RN

Routledge is an imprint of the Taylor & Francis Group, an informa business

Library of Congress Cataloging in Publication Data
Names: Gorlewski, Julie A., author.
Title: English language arts : a critical introduction / Julie Gorlewski.
Description: New York, NY : Routledge, 2018. | Includes bibliographical
references and index.
Identifiers: LCCN 2018001265 | ISBN 9781138721128 (hardback : alk. paper) |
ISBN 9781138721142 (pbk. : alk. paper) | ISBN 9781315194691 (ebook)
Subjects: LCSH: Language arts. | English language--Study and teaching. |
Teachers--Training of. | Curriculum planning.
Classification: LCC LB1576 .G7218 2018 | DDC 372.6--dc23
LC record available at https://lccn.loc.gov/2018001265

ISBN: 978-1-138-72112-8 (hbk)
ISBN: 978-1-138-72114-2 (pbk)
ISBN: 978-1-315-19469-1 (ebk)

Typeset in Bembo
by Taylor & Francis Books

For all the English teachers, past, present, and future, whose love of language and learners creates endless ripples of change in the world.

CONTENTS

ILLUSTRATIONS

Figures

Tables

Box

INTRODUCTION

Teaching matters. And, because language is intimately interconnected with thinking, the ways in which language is taught and learned matters. Since much of our learning and thinking is wrapped within, saturated by, and replete with language, its significance cannot be overstated. English teachers, it can be argued, provide the foundation on which learning in all disciplines is built.

When I ask candidates and teachers why they have chosen this profession, they tend to talk about love – love of literature, love for young people, love for the practices of reading or writing. They rarely mention politics, power, or liberation. They never mention subversion. There are good reasons for these responses – reasons based on the lived experiences of those of us who choose to teach. Many of us who become English teachers don't love just literature and young people; we love *school*. After all, we have chosen a profession that likely means that we will spend most of our adult waking hours in a school. People choose to spend their lives in places where they feel comfortable, places filled with people and procedures that they trust, places where they feel smart, confident, and successful.

When I discuss this phenomenon with teachers and teacher candidates, I remind them that they – *we*, really, since I am an educator – are atypical. What feels like comfort and common sense to us does not reflect the experience of most learners in public schools, many of whom are alienated and oppressed by the hegemonic structures of school, the forced engagements with texts, and the hidden curriculum that reinforces existing power relations and produces self-blame for systemic failure.

In addition to its application in teaching and learning all disciplines, teaching English has two other unique features. One lies in the infinite range of texts it can consider as part of the field, and the second lies in the ways that language, culture, and identity intertwine as mutually constructive components of one another. Our thoughts are shaped by language and our experiences of the world; understandings of each other are influenced by language, and language reflects and produces culture and its related systems of power. English teachers, as facilitators of language learning, play a key role in all of these realms. English teachers can determine whether, in broad strokes, knowledge is defined as facts from authoritative sources (to be repeated by students through formatted responses) or knowledge is co-constructed with students creating meaning through and with relevant texts. This distinction is essential, and its duality frames and fills this book.

Theory and Practice

The duality named in the previous sentence may seem extreme. It is unlikely that anyone decides to become a teacher in order to help students restate authoritative texts in five-paragraph essays. However, it is also improbable that people choose to become teachers because they see it for the political work that it is. Like all professions, teaching is steeped in tradition and culture, and these traditions and cultures can be explained and understood through social theory. Instead of focusing primarily on the intent of the practices we enact and the decisions we make, we can use social theories to situate our practices and decisions. This begins with understandings of theoretical perspectives related to education.

The examples named earlier can reveal how this works. A teacher who practices with a **functionalist** ideology, even if this ideology is not consciously identified, sees knowledge as existing in a traditional canon and the role of English teacher to impart academic skills to students. In essence, the content remains stable regardless of the context of the classroom and the nature of the learners. From this stance, as noted earlier, knowledge is defined as facts from authoritative sources to be repeated by students through formatted responses. In contrast, a teacher whose practices correspond to a **critical theoretical** perspective, even if it is not conscious or stated, is likely to construct knowledge *with* students, based on their own cultural experiences. Such a teacher will recognize that academic English is an arbitrarily defined category that reflects and perpetuates existing hegemonic relations, and will center the language and thinking of students in creating learning experiences. For this teacher, content is fluid and flexible, and skills are honed through analysis of texts that speak to and are derived from local and global communities.

It is, of course, easy to caricature both practices – the former as archaic and the latter as radical. However, this polarity can be concealed in the everyday, common-sense exercises of schooling. The concealment suppresses possibilities for transformation and enhances the likelihood that existing practices will be replicated, thus reproducing inequities. Although popular rhetoric dismisses the relevance of theory, theory represents a lever for justice. Theory enables us to question the status quo, to examine our assumptions, and to work toward liberation in our everyday classroom practice. As the adage goes, *Nothing is as practical as a good theory*.

There is a school of thought in which a triangle of relationships marks teaching. This triangle illustrates two possible relationships of power in teaching: teachers and content versus students, or students and teachers versus content. In the field of English education, our content can be described as "texts," so this choice can be reconceived as teachers and texts versus students, or students and teachers versus texts. Contemporary critical theory rejects both, instead calling for an approach in which students, and teachers, consume and produce texts, constructing meanings that reveal and reject oppression and moving society toward equity and justice.

Although sociological theories may seem esoteric, and far removed from classroom realities, even the simplest illustrations can expose beliefs related to theoretical perspectives. For example, theories of literature, or beliefs about how texts relate to readers, influence how literature is taught. Similarly, beliefs about the purposes and practices of writing affect how teachers approach writing instruction.

This volume will apply critical theoretical perspectives to teaching English language arts by considering how meanings are made in the intersecting spaces of learners, teachers, and texts. Enduring tensions in the field of English education will be explored and then contextualized in contemporary conditions to reveal how relations of power are constructed, (re)produced, and consumed. This book will contemplate the role of language in creating texts and norms as well as in resisting and transforming. The critical lens that frames and magnifies these ideas will reveal both the inherently political nature of teaching and the essential possibilities of transformation that exist in the praxis of theory and practice.

A critical theoretical perspective privileges questions over answers, doubt over certainty, and struggle over solutions. Critical theory, through a dialogic approach that toggles between microscopic and telescopic lenses, can expose how relations of power function at multiple levels including through personal interactions, in institutional settings, and scaled in larger social, even global, milieus. Further, a critical pedagogical standpoint requires teachers to develop curriculum in concert with learners, a strategy that is particularly applicable to English language arts. Language, as a component of culture, influences all aspects of education. English teachers have a unique responsibility, and a real obligation, to create opportunities for learners to cultivate literacy practices that will empower them to reach their potential.

Structure of the Book

Chapter 1, *What Does it Mean to Teach English Language Arts?* takes a bird's eye view of the field, considering its origins and its prospects. It introduces a critical perspective, defines key terms, and asks teachers and candidates to reflect on their own experiences and imagine how these experiences might affect their approach to the profession. Chapter 2, *Who Are Learners and Teachers, Really?* explores beliefs about learners, teachers, and schools, as well as how these beliefs affect classrooms. Focusing on equity and diversity, the chapter examines different models of teaching as well as various types of standards that influence curriculum. Chapter 3, *Curriculum in English Classrooms: Who Should Decide?* presents curriculum as a set of decisions. This perspective illuminates the sociocultural nature of curriculum and the ways that power is exercised in schools and classrooms. In Chapter 4, *How Can We Teach Texts in Context?* various conceptions of the literary canon are discussed. Theories of literature, and how these theories affect instruction, are presented, and distinctions between literacy and literature are investigated. Chapter 5, *Being and Becoming Writers: Who Can Be an Author?* emphasizes the interconnectedness of writing and thinking. Distinctions between writing as a product and writing as a process are discussed, as is the role of assessment in the development of writing identity. Chapter 6, *The Politics of Teaching: Are Teachers Agents of the State or Agents of Change?* underscores the political nature of teaching, illuminating the role of teacher as public intellectual. The chapter highlights English classrooms as spaces of possibility by accentuating professional dilemmas as opportunities for cultivating critical dispositions.

Each chapter begins with a scenario that demonstrates how the concepts play out in real classrooms. In every case, the scenarios were modeled on actual school experiences. To facilitate analysis of the cases, readers may wish to use the ExPAND framework provided in Appendix A.

To enhance understanding, vocabulary that may be unfamiliar is bold, and all bolded terms are defined in the Glossary of Terms, provided in Appendix B. Chapters conclude with extension questions designed to reveal and expand on how the concepts presented connect theory and practice.

1

WHAT DOES IT MEAN TO TEACH ENGLISH LANGUAGE ARTS?

Disheartened, Yolanda read her department chair's notes on the lesson plan she had submitted last week. Based on the novel The Great Gatsby, *Yolanda had created a vocabulary lesson that incorporated many of the best practices she had learned in her teacher education program. Her plan included activation of students' prior knowledge and the allocation of class time for guided practice. It also included expectations for students to make real-world applications of the terms. Her department chair's comments, however, seemed to ignore the careful scaffolding of vocabulary instruction and the multimodal approaches to engaging students with the assigned terms. Yolanda was particularly proud of her assessment plan, which linked to the learning objectives and offered students choices about how to show what they had learned. Instead of focusing on the lesson structure or content, her department chair posed a series of questions: "Is this list from the board-approved vocabulary list for this grade level? Why are these terms important for students to learn? Who selected these terms, and why? What terms were omitted, and why? How is this content relevant to students' development as consumers and producers of texts?" Frustrated, Yolanda wondered how to answer these questions, and whether the answers even mattered.*

What does it mean to teach English? What has it meant in the past, what does it mean today, and what might it mean in the future? How is teaching English different from, and similar to, acquiring language? And why does teaching English matter?

These questions, and the infinite questions that emerge from and around them, guide the work of English teachers. They undergird our decisions, shape our relationships with learners, and determine the trajectories of our careers. Such questions are also consistent with a critical approach to education, which focuses on questions, relations of power, and the ongoing struggles over the purposes of education. The social purposes and contexts of education are traditionally explored in foundations of education; however, as aspiring teachers focus on methods of instruction and lesson planning, connections between the essential questions of practice fade into the background and often dissolve within the everyday demands of teaching. This book seeks to address that imbalance and to foreground the importance of *why* we do what we do so that the *why's* establish the *what's* and the *how's* of our work. Because teaching is complex and challenging, and the needs of learners are urgent, it is common to concentrate on the immediate – on lesson plans that are due, on assignments to be assessed, and on the learners before us. But a lens that remains microscopic and fails to consider the broader contexts in which we act, however well intended, is insufficient. To be transformative, to work toward justice through education, teachers must practice through a lens that incorporates microscopic *and* telescopic perspectives, simultaneously recognizing the tensions of our practice and the need to engage with learners in the present.

This chapter will explore how the field of English language arts is defined and practiced through the experiences of teachers and learners. The reason that the field is contested mirrors the inherent tensions of our pluralistic society in which different people have different ideas about what it means to teach English.

Many aspiring teachers seek to become professionals in settings that are similar to those in which they were educated; they may want to create classrooms that replicate the strengths of the classrooms they loved as students. In English language arts (ELA), this often means that teacher candidates look forward to teaching the texts that drew them to the career. Instead of investigating the meaning of ELA and imagining change, candidates may envision teaching reading, writing, speaking, and listening in classrooms that replicate their own schooling. Some prospective teachers have been taught that there is a canon of the best literary works and that their task is to transmit this culture of human literary excellence to their students. Still others believe that the primary role of the ELA teacher is to provide the tools for future workplace productivity. Yet others believe that ELA is political in that what and how we read and write represents particular interests and promotes particular ways of seeing and being in the world. In this critical perspective, the stories we tell and the ways we tell them matter in terms of who gains access to resources and who gets valued or devalued socially. These disagreements about what an ELA teacher should believe and do are not merely individual. There are patterns to understanding how and why people have these different ideas.

This chapter begins by examining the assumptions and beliefs that underlie the field of ELA and then introduces a critical perspective. The chapter will discuss how professional organizations, policymakers, educational scholars, and practitioners define the purposes and practices of ELA. Careful consideration of what lies behind meanings and definitions is essential. Therefore, implicit and explicit definitions of terms such as ELA, literature, literacy, discourse, pedagogy, and critical theory will be presented and contextualized in terms of their political origins and implications. The chapter will conclude with a set of guiding questions designed to help readers compare and contrast definitions of the field in relation to the beliefs and assumptions that support them.

What Does It Mean to Teach English Language Arts?

The question *What does it mean to teach English language arts?* is really two questions: *What does it mean to teach?*, and *What is the curriculum of English language arts?* Each question is broad and complex, involving interlocking sets of decisions. Wondering about the meaning of teaching illustrates contested beliefs about purposes of school, especially public schools, which are supported by public funds and are therefore answerable to society. It seems obvious that the purpose of public education is to promote the needs of the society that supports it. However, an exploration of this apparently obvious purpose reveals dilemmas. One such dilemma involves whether public schools should support aspects of a society that are unjust. Historically, public schools have served as **social mechanisms** of both mobility and of oppression. While stories of education as a part of a system of **meritocracy** are familiar, schools are also systems that perpetuate inequities of the status quo. For example, in the US, Native children were forced to attend boarding schools where their language and culture were forbidden. Educators, by enacting oppressive policies, enabled children to be abused, families to be shattered, and generations of cultural heritage to be erased. Still today, children whose home culture does not correspond with school culture can experience education as discriminatory.

It is unlikely that anyone would suggest that schools ought to promote inequity; most people would agree that one purpose of education is to provide opportunities for everyone to contribute meaningfully to society. However, the conflicting purposes of education emerge in these examples. Schools, which reflect society with all its positive and negative characteristics, are expected to both prepare students for a society that exists, and prepare them to construct a more just and equitable world. If society were equitable, there would be no conflict between educating for the status quo and educating for justice; and transformation would be unnecessary. However, because inequities exist, a critical theoretical perspective is necessary. **Critical theory**, which remains by its very nature a contested concept, emerged from a school of thought that involves questioning relations of power. This also involves interrogating how categories of knowledge, including language, are constructed, produced, and reproduced. A critical approach to education intentionally and systematically makes injustice visible. Because it exposes institutional inequities, and schools are institutions, critical education jeopardizes the established existence of the organizations through which it occurs. By raising questions that lead to action, critical education represents change.

Purposes and Practices of English Language Arts

Teaching and learning are complex, intensely human undertakings. Teaching English, teaching about language arts through the arts of language, is relentlessly reflective; to a tremendous extent, we use language to teach and learn language.

The term **English language arts** is itself emblematic of how the field is defined and practiced. "English" is primary; its capitalization and primacy reveals a perspective about content. Despite and through its colonial origins, English has become an informal official language in the US. The unexamined acceptance of this condition conceals the effects of colonization: thefts of Indigenous land, enslavement of disproportionately Black and Brown bodies, and attempted erasure of oppressed cultures. Mandated standardized tests reinforce the dominance of English in US classrooms, since students must demonstrate proficiency in English to earn a high school diploma. Historically, this was not always true; in the early 20th century instruction often occurred in the language that was predominant in the community. "English," then, would have been a core content area, much like math or history. The "arts" in ELA emphasizes the literary and linguistic elements that underpin the field. Traditional debates regarding how the field is defined center on literature, involving questions such as *What types of literature need to be studied? How are acceptable genres determined? What literature belongs in the canon?* Similar questions address debates around teaching and learning linguistic aspects of language, such as *(How) should grammar be taught? What are essential literacy skills?* The term that identifies the field, ELA, is brimming with history, culture, and meanings that often remain unexamined, even by those in the field. It is worth wondering whether "English" is itself content, how its primacy as both content and means of instruction influences learning, and whether the arts of language are elite or inclusive.

Literature, Literacy, and Pedagogy

For English teachers, the "what" of teaching, or the content of our classrooms, consists of texts and skills related to consuming and producing texts. **Literature** refers to the texts read as part of the ELA curriculum. **Literacy** refers to the skills necessary to consume and produce multiple genres of texts. As noted earlier, both aspects are contested. Asking one hundred English teachers to identify ten texts every high school graduate should read will yield hundreds of results. Professional organizations and policymakers publish lists of recommended texts, but these serve as guidelines that continuously evolve as new texts are published and a wider array of perspectives are involved in such decisions. Historically, the canon of literature that dominated English classrooms was primarily white, male, and European/American – mirroring the political and economic power structure in which schools functioned. Literature anthologies reflected the canon of colonialism – and many still do. However, awareness of the oppressive nature of a colonial perspective, which idealizes some identities while marginalizing others, has resulted in a more inclusive understanding of what texts matter, and whose stories are worthy of being read. Similar struggles surround the teaching and learning of skills related to consuming and producing texts. English classrooms generally privilege academic language. Teachers and texts dedicated to grammar and usage act to correct uses of language that do not conform with academic norms. This role of teachers and textbooks is consistent with the purpose of school as a means of assimilation; however, this approach to teaching English can also serve to alienate learners whose home language does not match the language of school. An inclusive approach to both text content and related skills can address the needs of learners without lowering standards or diminishing expectations.

Essential to conceptions of ELA in schools are the methods and practices of teaching, or **pedagogy**. This returns us to the question of what it means to teach, leading to considerations about the roles of teachers and learners. Pedagogical theories address how teachers and learners interact with one another, as well as how they engage with the content and skills of **curriculum**. Curriculum can be defined narrowly as a list of content, or broadly as a course of study. Drawing on the work of Parkay, Hass, and Anctil, Fenwick English notes that definitions of "curriculum" tend to involve three categories: designation of content, learning outcomes, and "virtually all of the experiences a student might have in school" (10).

Curriculum, Student Achievement, and Accountability

Curriculum – through testing – can also be used as a means of **accountability**, or as a way of ensuring that expectations are met, responsibility for results is accepted, and results are reported. Political leaders seek to ensure that public schools, funded by tax dollars, are meeting the expectations of stakeholders. This is perceived as a way of holding educators accountable for their work. To that end, tests are given at regular intervals to evaluate the extent to which content and skills are being learned and developed. When curriculum is imposed by external entities through **standardized assessments**, the definition of curriculum becomes narrowed:

> Control is central to accountability. Most notions of accountability, especially those embodied in legislation that are punitive or remunerative, assume that school personnel are *in control* or *can control* [emphases in original] those factors that will lead to improved test performance. For this reason, the definition of curriculum is that it consists of any document or plan that exists in a school or school system that defines the work of teachers, at least to the extent of identifying the content to be taught children and the possible methods to be used in the process.
>
> *(English, 10)*

Limitations of this approach to school and teacher accountability are numerous. As English explains, standardized tests fail to consider **out-of-school factors** that may affect student performance. David Berliner identifies six out-of-school factors, or OSFs, that can affect the learning opportunities of children and potentially limit the ability of teachers and students to facilitate academic achievement. OSFs particularly relevant for children from communities marked by poverty include:

> (1) low birth-weight and non-genetic prenatal influences on children; (2) inadequate medical, dental, and vision care, often a result of inadequate or no medical insurance; (3) food insecurity; (4) environmental pollutants; (5) family relations and family stress; and (6) neighborhood characteristics.
>
> *(Berliner, 1)*

An additional concern about using standardized tests as a means of curricular accountability involves myths of objectivity that surround and undergird these assessments. Historically, standardized assessments have been used to maintain systems of power and oppression, reinforcing dominant narratives about what it means to be intelligent, articulate, and educated. Developed and implemented by the academic and cultural elite, standardized assessments have contributed to ideas of racism, sexism, and classicism; mass standardized testing continues to reflect and reinforce social hierarchies related to race, gender, and class. From kindergarten screening to SAT scores to GRE results, standardized assessments act as **gatekeepers** to academic achievement and professional opportunities. Despite a wealth of evidence revealing deleterious effects of such assessments, they continue to be used as a measure of school and teacher accountability.

Of course, teachers are accountable to learners, to communities, and to society, and public school teachers should be able to demonstrate the results of their classroom practice. From a critical perspective, in which assumptions are continuously questioned, it would be beneficial to ask: *To whom are teachers accountable?* And, *To whom are schools accountable?* If policymakers mandate curriculum linked to accountability measures that could negatively influence the prospects of learners, should teachers be accountable to policymakers or to learners? If needs conflict, should teachers follow directives of political leaders or community members? Scores on standardized tests provide one method of assessing accountability toward meeting certain instructional goals, but other curricular goals require different kinds of **assessment** associated with learning objectives that are less linear and more difficult to quantify.

Given the role of education in shaping society, many education scholars use the term "curriculum" to mean everything that teachers teach and everything that learners learn in school. This definition includes the "**hidden curriculum**" of behavior, expectations, and unspoken understandings of what it means to be educated. The hidden curriculum is distinct from the written curriculum that is published and intentionally presented in classrooms. The hidden curriculum is unofficial, involving norms, values, and messages about what expectations and perspectives are related to academic achievement, power, and status in educational institutions. Aspects of the hidden curriculum are transmitted through classroom practices, instructional strategies, disciplinary policies, extracurricular offerings, and institutional structures. For example, classrooms where students sit in rows and speak when called on by the teacher transmit the message that communication is controlled by an authority figure. Likewise, decisions about content reflect a hidden curriculum: What authors are assigned? What books are available to students? What topics are appropriate for research projects? Extra-curricular activities provide a glimpse into the hidden curricula, as well. Particular sets of values are perpetuated when football games are celebrated by cheerleaders and assemblies, while swim meets and soccer games are unacknowledged. The hidden curriculum also illuminates the negative spaces related to curricular decisions – that is, what is missing from school life. Often, activities such as dance, skateboarding, and hip-hop are absent from the daily lives of students in school, even though they are powerful influences on the out-of-school lives of youth.

A critical theoretical perspective of curriculum recognizes it as a series of decisions made by various stakeholders. Such decisions are best made in close proximity to and even in consultation with, students. Typically, however, standards-based curricula involve curricular decisions that hold students and teachers accountable for achievement without consideration of the context – the OSFs that affect student performance, as well as the historical biases of standardized assessment. Figure 1.1 illustrates how the public perceives student achievement, and Figure 1.2 reveals the complex interactions of curriculum, assessment, and student achievement.

Taken together, these graphics demonstrate the differing levels of control that teachers and students have over curricular decisions for which they are held accountable. Curricular decisions represent in-school factors that influence student performance.

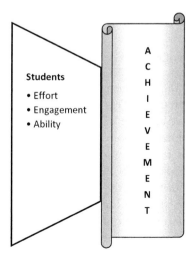

FIGURE 1.1 Traditional perspective of factors related to student achievement

Students	Parents/Families	School Environment	Curriculum	Teachers	ACHIEVEMENT

• Effort
• Engagement
• Ability
	• Socio-Economic Status
	• Culture
	• Native Language
	• Education
	  • Background knowledge
	  • Experiences
	  • Self-confidence
	  • Faith in system
	• Support
	  • Time
	  • Nutrition
	  • Extracurricular opportunity
	• Home
	  • Place to study
	  • Materials
	  • Academic help when necessary
		• Facilities
		• Quality
		  • Heat/Air conditioning
		  • Light
		  • Air
		  • Aesthetics
		  • Security
		  • Daily Schedule
		• Instructional materials
		  • Texts
		  • Technologies
		  • Athletics
		  • Arts
		  • Sciences
		• Organizational Culture
		  • Leadership
		  • Student Population
		• Institutional Support
		  • Extra help
		  • Enrichment
		  • Student/Family Services
			• Standards
			  • Current
			  • Relevant
			• Content
			  • Prior Knowledge
			  • Cultural Connections
			  • Bias
			  • Level of Significance
			• Level of Cognitive Engagement
			• Amount of Information
			• Conceptual Validity
			• High-Stakes Assessment
				• Quality
				  • Certification
				  • Level of Preparation
				  • Ongoing Professional Development
				• Instructional implementation
				  • Lesson Planning
				  • Assignments
				  • Assessments
				  • Ongoing Feedback
				• Student/Family Relations
				  • Communication
				  • Multicultural perspective	

FIGURE 1.2 A fuller picture of factors related to student achievement

Decisions about curriculum connect with pedagogy because what is taught matters as much as how it is taught. Teachers employ similar curricula with different pedagogical approaches, resulting in differing student experiences. A traditional pedagogical approach emphasizes basic skills, textbooks, and repetition of accepted information. The role of teachers in a traditional pedagogical framework is to break down information and deliver it to students, then offer opportunities for practicing proven skills that reinforce content. A **constructivist** pedagogical approach is based on the idea that learners construct meanings, often in collaborative settings, based on extension of prior knowledge. In a classroom with a constructivist approach, teachers and students might work together to develop curriculum. Constructivist pedagogies tend to be project-based and emphasize inquiry. Building on the ideas of constructivism through critical theory, critical pedagogies move from individual questions about content to consider how social institutions such as schools influence relations of power in society.

Critical theory, unlike traditional social theories which seek to explain society, focuses on questioning assumptions and effecting change. Critical theory is grounded in deep understandings of history and culture, and emphasizes investigations of how political and economic structures shape identities, social relations, and societal institutions. An essential feature of critical theory is its dual nature; it is expected to explain social problems and effect change necessary to address them. A classroom dedicated to **critical pedagogies** involves teachers and students working together to examine social problems, investigate root causes, and generate solutions. All these examples of pedagogies involve content and skills; the difference between them involves the central focus through which content and skills are taught and learned. This focus affects the roles of teachers and students as content and skills are developed. These roles can be perceived as points on a continuum that span various levels of control and autonomy, as well as perspectives regarding the role of schools in perpetuating current norms versus changing society.

Discourse and the Profession of English Education

Despite the complications revealed by close consideration of what it means to teach ELA, many approach this work with a relatively straightforward conception of the task. This section will discuss how policymakers, professional organizations, and scholars influence the field. Each of these groups (and there are, of course, intersections of membership among them) participates in the creation and uses of discourses that define the field.

In the sociology of education, the term **discourse** is more than surface-level communication. Discourses operate throughout societies, affecting identity construction and perpetuating power relations through everyday activities of cultural participants. Ways of being, thinking, and knowing are governed by discursive forces which are perceived as natural and normal – common sense – and can thus proceed unquestioned. Emerging from and ultimately contributing to ideologies, or worldviews, discourse involves interrelations among knowledge, thought, and communication. Our worldviews shape what we know, and this knowledge affects how social institutions are structured. All of these interactions are influenced by power, because discourses are embedded in, and emerge from, relations of power.

Discourse involves how we organize our thoughts, which influence understandings of our world. For example, for someone who is familiar with baseball, terms such as "full count" and "double play" are resonant and meaningful. A musician understands the words "bar," "measure," and "beat" in specific ways that differ from colloquial usage. These examples reveal how discourse emerges from institutions (sports and music) and provide structure and order for concepts and experiences. Concepts are named and connected with shared experiences, both formal and informal, over time. Discourses are created and perpetuated in universities, in corporations, in country clubs and in prisons. Discourse shapes thoughts, feelings, behaviors, and interactions with others. Discourses are cultural, contextual, and they operate as mechanisms of inclusion and exclusion. As a sociocultural phenomenon, discourse operates to make some ways of thinking and being seem right, natural, and normal, while alternate ways of thinking and being seem improper or offensive. Consequences associated with discourse are significant and far-reaching, and critical approaches to English teaching involve analysis of how discourses are produced and consumed inside and outside of classrooms. Such analysis might begin with consideration of how hidden curricula function within classrooms and schools.

Policymakers often define English education as preparation for the workforce, and see the role of teachers as ensuring that graduates can contribute as productive members of society. Professional organizations serve several important purposes. First, they provide historical context for the profession, enabling teachers to trace how their work has been defined and experienced. They also serve as liaisons between educators and policymakers, amplifying the voices of teachers and interpreting them for state and federal officials. The cultural and historical contexts in the field of English lean toward tradition, and while advocacy is a significant aspect of their work, professional organizations tend to reinforce existing roles and categories. Professional organizations, including unions, provide opportunities for teachers to come together to develop position statements for policymakers, create guidelines for teachers, and disseminate publications that improve practice. Similarly, English education scholars are acculturated into the discourse of the field first, and then are expected to extend knowledge through research and publication. Accreditors rely on standards developed by professional organizations, so college and university programs are impacted greatly by these standards. It is evident that the work of policymakers, professional organizations, and scholars intersect in ways that deeply influence the lives of teachers and students.

The role of English teachers in an educational system that is heavily influenced by standards and regulations is twofold. English teachers endeavor to cultivate linguistic fluency so that learners can contribute to society. At the same time, English teachers are expected to facilitate a critical approach to the discourses of power in society to ensure that all learners have equal opportunities to contribute. Native discourses must be valued even as academic discourses are developed, consumed, and produced. Academic discourses must be simultaneously cultivated and interrogated. A classroom focusing solely on success in today's world might unintentionally foreclose possibilities for some learners; therefore, it is incumbent on teachers to collaborate with learners to uncover mechanisms of oppression as they manifest in texts, in educational institutions, in classroom interactions, and in society as a whole.

Through critical pedagogical approaches that unpack systems of oppression while engaging students in authentic curricular experiences, English teachers can address the needs of learners today as well as achieve the goal of constructing a more just society tomorrow.

Summary

This chapter explored definitions of curriculum and pedagogy, and how theoretical constructs play out through classrooms. Definitions of literature and literacy were contextualized as socially constructed and related to differing power relations. Discussions involved power, culture, discourse, critical theory, critical pedagogy, and how professional organizations contribute to shaping the field. In addition, conflicting roles of teachers were considered as related to the sociocultural, historical contexts in which they work.

Extension Questions

1. Recall a classroom experience you have had. How did this experience align with the pedagogical theories briefly described in the chapter (traditional, constructivist, critical)?
2. The chapter discusses how content and pedagogies interrelate in classrooms. Consider how a curriculum focused on traditional canonical texts might be approached from a critical perspective. Is this possible? Why or why not? Describe how such an approach might look.
3. Reflect on your own experiences of learning in various settings. How did aspects of a "hidden curriculum" emerge? What were the unspoken rules and expectations, and how did they influence you?
4. Professional organizations and policymakers publish lists of texts to guide teachers in making selections for learners. Are these lists beneficial or harmful? Explain. Obtain a list and review the recommendations. What should be eliminated? What is missing?
5. English teachers are expected to demonstrate respect for multicultural discourses while also promoting academic discourse. Which of these aims is primary? Why? What factors determine this priority?

Works Cited

Berliner, David C. *Poverty and Potential: Out-of-School Factors and School Success.* Education Policy Research Unit, 2009. http://nepc.colorado.edu/publication/poverty-and-potential.

English, Fenwick W. *Deciding What to Teach and Test: Developing, Aligning, and Leading the Curriculum.* Newbury Park, CA: Corwin, 2010.

Parkay, Forrest W., Eric J. Antil, and Glenn Hass. *Curriculum Leadership: Readings for Developing Quality Educational Programs.* Boston, MA: Allyn & Bacon, 2010.

2

WHO ARE LEARNERS AND TEACHERS, REALLY?

"Get out." Keisha Williams locked eyes with the student and pointed to the door. "Wait for me in the office." In the silent classroom, Stacey rose, slammed her books into a pile, and stalked out of the classroom, her every movement followed by the eyes of her peers and teacher.

Suppressing frustration, Keisha continued the class, although she and her students were noticeably subdued. When the bell rang and her class emptied, Keisha went to the office to meet Stacey.

"I'm going to have to write a referral," Keisha explained.

"Whatever; who cares?" Stacey brushed past her and left the office.

"What was that?" Alyson, who had almost collided with Stacey, asked her colleague.

Keisha groaned, pulling a referral from the drawer. "That girl is a nightmare! Every day is a new issue. She is impossible – disruptive, disrespectful, and refuses to do any work!"

Alyson stared from the referral to Keisha's face. "Wait – you're writing a referral? I've never seen you write up a student, ever! And for Stacey – that sweet girl in my fourth period class? She is one of my favorite students. In fact, she helped design my bulletin board last week."

"We can't be talking about the same student!" Keisha and Alyson shared a puzzled glance. One thing was certain: they needed to talk.

Making the Familiar Strange

Most teachers, and teacher candidates, have spent many years in formal education. Furthermore, people who become teachers tend to have been successful in these institutions. To enter the profession, teachers have earned diplomas, undergraduate and sometimes graduate degrees, and certifications. These conditions are meant to ensure that educators are well prepared and highly qualified. However, they also serve as a means of reproduction and acculturation. When teachers, or any specialists, are inducted into a profession, they cultivate assumptions and perspectives that shape their worldviews. These **assumptions**, or unexamined beliefs that shape perceptions and practices, influence attitudes teachers have toward schools, disciplinary content, and learners. To qualify for a teacher education program, students graduate high school and enroll in college. Then, they must maintain a competitive grade point average. These gatekeepers, alone, restrict the transformative nature of the profession; students who are not successful in the *current* system have limited, or no, voice in effecting change.

Teacher candidates tend to believe in the systems that produced them. This is a natural tendency, reinforced by social, institutional, and professional norms. However, it also results in educators who may be unlikely to question assumptions about teaching, learning, and schools. Because many people spent a great deal of time during their formative years in education systems, beliefs about roles of participants in such systems are deeply held and often unexamined. In short, unfamiliar cultural contexts prompt us to interrogate conventions, but familiar contexts are difficult to examine. One purpose of this chapter is to develop the capacity to do what 18th-century German poet Novalis (as quoted in Rosen) described as "making the familiar strange" (174). This concept, widely referenced in relation to literature and curriculum, emphasizes the importance of how cultural practices, such as literacy, are socially constructed. As we are immersed in these practices, however, they begin to seem natural and normal, so we tend not to question or examine them. This chapter will reveal, categorize, and explore the roots and results of common beliefs – or **assumptions** – about teachers and learners. It will reveal assumptions, consider their implications, and explore how critical pedagogical approaches can influence educational consequences. Key terms introduced and discussed include "tabula rasa," epistemology, colonialism, banking model, Standard Academic English (SAE), standards, and culturally sustaining pedagogy.

Perspectives of learners and teachers are connected to overarching theories of knowledge, or **epistemologies**. An epistemology refers to the field of study related to the nature of knowledge, what counts as knowledge, methods of justification of knowledge, and beliefs derived from knowledge. For teachers, understanding the discourses and epistemologies that exist in the schools where they work is essential. As Oates states, "learning how to teach in (different) sites entailed acquiring a different literacy pedagogy, which for me meant taking on different views and beliefs about students, teachers, and the uses of written language" (1). This begins with the understanding that teaching English is a complex practice that requires analysis of how teachers and students are perceived in relation to language and literature.

Students and teachers can be perceived primarily as consumers of authoritative texts. Their main role is to replicate dominant discourse and reproduce existing practices. From this perspective, students are apprentice users of academic English. The role of teachers as professionals in the discipline is to deliver established literary knowledge to, and cultivate literacy skills in, the next generation of scholars and citizens. In contrast to these perspectives, or perhaps along a continuum of advocacy and justice, is a critical perspective of the roles of learners and teachers. A critical perspective of the learning process partners teachers and learners as co-producers of knowledge. Rather than partially complete adults or apprentice users of thought and language, learners are perceived as participants in the process – as capable thinkers and communicators with ideas that are valuable in and of themselves. Instead of accepting and transmitting established knowledge, teachers create classrooms in which knowledge is constructed, authority is questioned, power relations are revealed, and injustices are interrupted. In such settings, students and teachers are perceived first as active creators of meanings and texts, creators whose encounters with language produce changes in culture and discourse.

This chapter will explore how these perspectives connect policy and practice to the lives of teachers and learners. Throughout this chapter, intersections and overlapping aspects of these categories will be emphasized and made concrete. The chapter will conclude with a set of guiding questions designed to help readers compare and contrast conceptions of learners and teachers in relation to the beliefs and assumptions that support them.

Traditional Perspectives

One traditional perspective regards learners as "blank slates" that need to be filled with knowledge deemed relevant by authority figures such as teachers (or the state). This perception of students is derived from the term "**tabula rasa**," which translates from Latin into "scraped tablet" or "clean slate." A perception of students as blank slates implies that they are born into the world, and ultimately arrive in schools, with minimal or no knowledge about academic content. Learners' experiences in the family and community are presumed to be unrelated to school-based learning.

This perspective about learners influences how teachers teach, centering the teacher as the sole repository of knowledge from which learners can benefit. Teachers are positioned as authority figures who are charged to shape the identities of learners by structuring activities and instructional experiences that will enable students to know "truths" about the world. It is important to note that this is a pedagogical approach in which teachers teach and learners learn. As blank slates, learners are perceived as having nothing to offer in terms of ideas or original thoughts; they are conceived as being entirely open to the knowledge that is presented through experiences planned and implemented by teachers.

In English language arts, this perspective also influences how texts are used in classrooms. For example, the concept of students as "blank slates" conflicts with the concept that readers interact with text and construct meanings through active engagement. Likewise, writing is taught as an act that primarily involves repeating ideas based on experiences connected to authoritative sources. That is, if students do not possess original thoughts or ideas, their writing is reproductive rather than generative. Approaches to speaking and listening are similar in that listening is a receptive act designed to provide access to accepted knowledge, and speech is based on given content and adheres to specified models.

A similar epistemological perspective about teaching and learning is known as the "**banking model**" or "**transmission model**" of education. Comparable to "blank slates," students are perceived as "empty vessels" into which teachers transfer information. Educator and activist Paolo Freire, in his book *Pedagogy of the Oppressed*, critiqued this transmission model of education, which he referred to as the "banking model," because students were perceived as passive recipients of information, receptacles for deposits through instruction, which are ultimately withdrawn through assessments. Freire describes the banking model as consistent with methods involving rote memorization. Education is perceived as a narrated process, wherein teachers talk and students listen – as distinct from a dialogue in which both participants contribute. Freire explains:

> Narration (with the teacher as narrator) leads the students to memorize mechanically the narrated account. Worse yet, it turns them into "containers," into "receptacles" to be "filled" by the teachers. The more completely she fills the receptacles, the better a teacher she is. The more meekly the receptacles permit themselves to be filled, the better students they are.
>
> Education thus becomes an act of depositing, in which the students are the depositories and the teacher is the depositor. Instead of communicating, the teacher issues communiques and makes deposits which the students patiently receive, memorize, and repeat. This is the "banking" concept of education, in which the scope of action allowed to the students extends only as far as receiving, filing, and storing the deposits. (71–72)

Expanding his discussion of the roles of teacher and student, Freire notes that:

> In the banking concept of education, knowledge is a gift bestowed by those who consider themselves knowledgeable upon those whom they consider to know nothing. Projecting an absolute ignorance onto others, a characteristic of the ideology of oppression, negates education and knowledge as processes of inquiry. (72)

The transmission, or banking, model offers a dichotomous perspective of a complex set of roles; however, it also offers a framework from which we can examine classroom practice. The polarity of principles Freire uses to describe the banking model is useful in this way. According to Freire, in a banking model of education:

a   the teacher teaches and the students are taught;
b   the teacher knows everything and the students know nothing;

c   the teacher thinks and the students are thought about;

d   the teacher talks and the students listen – meekly;

e   the teacher disciplines and the students are disciplined;

f   the teacher chooses and enforces his choice, and the students comply;

g   the teacher acts and the students have the illusion of acting through the action of the teacher;

h   the teacher chooses the program content, and the students (who were not consulted) adapt to it;

i   the teacher confuses the authority of knowledge with his or her own professional authority, which she and he sets in opposition to the freedom of the students;

j   the teacher is the Subject of the learning process, while the pupils are mere objects. (73)

The role of teachers, then, is to transmit accepted knowledge (that is, knowledge that corresponds with dominant discourses in society) and assess the extent to which learners absorb it. Examples of accepted knowledge emerge when we imagine expectations for what an educated person might know, such as awareness of the first president of the United States, or the mathematical operation associated with the plus sign. Additional illustrations of accepted knowledge abound in English language arts: the author of *Romeo and Juliet*, the written symbol for an interrogative phrase or clause, the structure of a five-paragraph persuasive essay. Although what constitutes accepted knowledge is contested, its cultural prominence remains powerful. Those who view public education as a means of transmitting accepted knowledge see learners as "pre-adults," or as individuals whose primary purpose is to prepare for the next phase in their lives. Adherents to this type of belief imagine the purpose of schools and teachers is to ensure that young people are "college and career ready" upon graduation. The role of teachers, then, is to train students to serve as productive members of the economy. Learners are passive recipients; and the professionalism of teachers varies depending on the extent to which they can determine the knowledge and skills that are taught, the methods of instruction, and the ways learners are assessed.

Traditional perspectives of teaching and learning, such as the transmission model, are emblematic of **colonialism**. As the term implies, colonialism is a phenomenon wherein a dominant entity overpowers and exerts control over an existing entity. Colonization can occur at many levels and through many practices, but it involves gaining influence over land, resources, and people, and then exploiting any or all of these for economic gain. Appropriation of land and confiscation of resources result in the displacement of people and affect culture, relationships, and access to wealth. Human bodies can become chattels when their labor is appropriated through slavery. Further, colonization, by influencing behavior, language, and education, affects learning and thinking. As an exercise of power, colonialism affirms the dominance of one group over another, and reinforces beliefs consistent with the righteousness of this dominance. Although beliefs and assumptions are significant aspects of colonialism, it is important to keep in mind what Tuck and Yang remind us: (de)colonization, although laden with conceptual meanings and implications, is *not* a metaphor. It has concrete, material consequences that affect the life experiences of individuals, the formation and operation of institutions, and the economic and political opportunities of peoples.

As social institutions, schools are involved in colonization. For example, a colonial approach to teaching asserts the value of particular forms of language. In most US schools, SAE that aligns with a set of prescribed rules is perceived as correct, and alternative forms of language are rejected. Students whose language use does not conform with SAE are routinely corrected, even when the language is rooted in home and community norms. Well-meaning teachers might imagine that they are providing students with access to SAE as the language of power in contemporary society; however, they are also imparting a hidden curriculum about linguistic value, and whose languages matter. Historically, schools in colonies stripped students of their native languages. This occurred when England colonized Ireland and India, and when American colonists seized Indigenous lands and forced children to attend boarding schools – among innumerable other examples. In these cases, linguistic colonization was obvious. Today, colonial influences may be more subtle, but in some classrooms implications are still visible. Making this point, Jamila Lyiscott first draws on Thiong'o, who upon reflecting on his schooling described the troubling realization that "the language of my education was no longer the language of my culture" (111). His language, a constituent component of thought, was occupied and displaced through education by the language of colonizers. Furthermore, because language is deeply intertwined with culture, when language is colonized, disciplinary content is colonized, as well. For example, positivist terminology frames how people think about science, but not all cultures approach science from a positivist perspective. Greg Cahete's definition of Indigenous perspectives of science reveals physical and metaphysical dimensions, and is clearly connected to what Western culture might define as literary ways of thinking:

> Native science is a metaphor for a wide range of tribal processes of perceiving, thinking, acting, and 'coming to know' that have evolved through human experience with the natural world. Native science is born of a lived and storied participation with the natural landscape. To gain a sense of Native science, one must participate with the natural world. To understand the foundations of Native science one must become open to the roles of sensation, perception, imagination, emotion, symbols, and spirit as well as that of concept, logic, and rational empiricism. (5)

The relationship between language and content is evident, and it is easy to see how using only SAE and Western science terminology would diminish cultural richness associated with Native science. Understanding these ideas is one thing; addressing them in the current context is another. Leigh Patel identifies the difficulties of being transformative within a system designed to reinforce the status quo. She explains:

> Since its inception in the United States, versus the pre-existing practices of Native peoples, formal schooling has had far more to do with the project of coloniality than it has with learning, teaching, or co-existence. This is not to say that learning and human growth doesn't happen frequently within schooling settings, but it is often the result of individuals who have committed themselves to swimming upstream, circumventing the design of schools as sites of discipline and social reproduction... (4)

Discourse, through language and culture, shapes pedagogical decisions that are enacted through explicit and hidden curricula. Colonial assumptions about how knowledge is produced and consumed, what knowledge is significant, whose texts are relevant, and how intelligence is evaluated through academic performance undergird traditional understandings of what it means to teach English. Colonial epistemologies reinforce perspectives of learners as empty vessels – passive absorbers of dominant knowledge – and of teachers as transmitters of both accepted information and unquestioned social norms.

Understanding the historical underpinnings of the educational system allows teachers to situate their work in contexts that encourage assumptions to be questioned. Questioning understandings about teaching, learning, language, and knowledge enriches teachers and develops the profession.

Students, Teachers, and Standards

Despite historical evidence of the role of educational institutions in reproducing inequities, many people in the US today believe that schools can provide a means of ensuring opportunity for all students. Contemporary reform initiatives tend to emphasize two approaches to curriculum development: standards-based and multicultural. While these are often presented as mutually exclusive, their differences center on definitions of knowledge and perceptions of the roles of learners and teachers. This section will discuss how a nuanced understanding of standards can create opportunities for critical pedagogies in standards-based curricula.

As standards dominate the educational landscape, it is important to realize that standards, themselves, are not standardized. Mueller differentiates between **content standards** (discipline-specific knowledge and skills), **process standards** (skills that strengthen the learning process, such as goal-setting), and **value standards** (attitudes that support learning, such as persistence). Further, standards are developed by many organizations for a variety of sometimes conflicting purposes.

A significant limitation of standards, however, is the focus on outcomes rather than inputs. Singular attention to outcomes conceals the contexts in which learning occurs. It obscures cultural mismatches between home and school, camouflages institutional inequities, and cloaks contextual inequities as "achievement gaps." Particular focus on outcomes gives an impression of equity by levelling expectations. However, this impression is incomplete. It ignores how curricular decisions are made and the importance of considering who decides. It ignores inequities of resource allocation, as well, disregarding both in-school and out-of-school contextual factors that affect student achievement. Consideration of these "inputs" points to what some scholars call "**opportunity-to-learn standards**." One example is offered by the National Council of Teachers of English (NCTE), which described the need for these standards at an interdisciplinary conference it sponsored in 1994.

> The opportunity to learn is the inherent right of every child in America. Educators, parents, and other members of a child's many communities share a common interest in the educational success of each child and in the role of education in our democratic society. Full, positive participation in democracy is contingent upon every child's access to quality education. Such access to high-quality education should not be dependent upon the specific community in which a child lives. By focusing and building upon the strengths of learners, Opportunity-to-learn standards can help ensure equitable access to high-quality education for all students in America.

In its statement, which NCTE reaffirmed in 2012, representatives noted that opportunity standards should provide:

- time for students to learn and reflect
- time for teachers to plan, teach, and reflect
- appropriate learning resources
- resources from the community

Unlike **outcomes-based standards**, opportunity-to-learn standards emphasize inputs related to resources for students, teachers, and communities. This stance reveals a perception of teachers and students as active participants in learning processes. Further, the focus on inputs and resources represents a systemic perspective of educational institutions and the communities they serve. That is, opportunity-to-learn standards portray student achievement as just one product of a large, complex system of in-school and out-of-school factors. Outcomes-based standards, in contrast, focus on demonstrable evidence of knowledge and skills. These types of standards offer, at best, a partial indicator of learning and accountability. By emphasizing results without consideration of input, outcome-based assessments reinforce a conception of learners as empty vessels while simultaneously ignoring the fact that some students' home lives afford them with greater access to experiences and tools related to academic success. Outcomes-based standards, coupled with the conception of students as empty vessels, work to assure the persistence of achievement inequities.

These differing perspectives of students, teachers, and educational institutions are significant because they shape how education is understood and enacted. Reigeluth explains that:

> ...standards can be used in two very different ways that represent very different views of education, each of which can be applied to any of the purposes described earlier. They can be used as tools for standardization – to help make all students alike. Or they can be used as tools for customization – to help meet individual students' needs. (202–203)

An outcomes-focused/standards-based approach to teaching and learning is consistent with recent federal legislation such as No Child Left Behind and Race to the Top. This approach is also evident in the widespread implementation of the Common Core Standards. Education systems based on standards-based curricula focus on the development of knowledge grounded in already-established norms of content-specific skills and expertise.

Standards, themselves, can be prescriptive or aspirational. **Prescriptive standards** are based on existing information, accepted facts, and predetermined decisions about content and skills. An example of prescriptive standards associated with predetermined expectations can be found in Common Core Standard CCSS. ELA-Literacy.L.8.2, related to *Conventions of Standard English*. This standard articulates the expectation that students will "Demonstrate command of the conventions of standard English capitalization, punctuation, and spelling when writing." Subsections of this standard indicate that students should be able to: "Use punctuation (comma, ellipsis, dash) to indicate a pause or break," "Use an ellipsis to indicate an omission," and "Spell correctly." The appeal of prescriptive standards is evident. They point to clear instructional goals that can be linked to easily measurable assessments, thereby simplifying lesson planning. It is easy to imagine how a teacher might develop a lesson in which students learn a set of rules about using an ellipsis to indicate an omission. The learning target is distinct, examples abound, and students can apply the knowledge and skill in numerous contexts. However, the learning standard, itself, is decontextualized. It is presented as part of the standards for grade 8, but it is possible that a writer might have occasion to use an ellipsis to show an omission in grade 5, or in grade 3. Alternatively, if students are taught the information in grade 8, but do not have the opportunity to apply the skill in an authentic writing experience until grade 10, skills may need to be relearned. That is, research indicates that conventions of writing are best taught in contexts that are meaningful and student-driven (Hillocks; Langer and Applebee). Spelling is another ostensibly straightforward aspect of instruction based on prescriptive standards. While written communication is often evaluated, in part, on the basis of whether spelling conforms with the rules of SAE, this is also a social construction. Efforts to standardize English have been traced as far back as the 12th century. Resulting systems have reflected the values of reformers, some of the most famous of whom have included Benjamin Franklin, Charles Darwin, Lord Tennyson, Mark Twain, and Theodore Roosevelt. In fact, an international organization known as The English Spelling Society, founded in 1908, continues to advocate for changes in spelling to create a system that is both uniform and equitable. Responding to a question about whether a more accessible spelling system equates to lowering standards, the society explains the elitist origins of 18th-century writer and lexicographer Samuel Johnson's attempt at standardization and describes the importance of an inclusive approach to literacy.

> *Isn't this dumbing down the language? Spelling said with the letter e (sed) and spelling done with the letter u (dun) looks ignorant and stupid.*
>
> We have all been conditioned to see these spellings as ignorant and stupid. In fact, in 1755, when Samuel Johnson published his dictionary which standardized our current spelling, his *purpose* was to set in stone tricks and traps in the form of irregularities so that only those in privileged positions could afford the time to learn them all. It was designed to be a way of distinguishing between the prestigious and the "riffraff".
>
> This attitude continues to prevail today, with spellings which accurately represent pronunciation being used in comics (*"sez yoo"*) and literature as the way that only the uneducated speak.
>
> In fact, the updated spelling would be much more intelligent and sensible than the system we have now.
>
> What is being proposed is not lowering the standard, but changing the standard so that more people can learn to read and write in less time, with less expense, and our children can get on to other subjects as quickly as children in other countries do. Democracy doesn't work with an uneducated, uninformed population.

Learners in English classrooms, regardless of their level of written language, are generally able to use language to communicate effectively. When language rules inhibit learners' confidence about their language practices, nascent linguistic identities are vulnerable. Fortunately, the converse is also true. Learners who are exposed to and engaged with critical approaches to language development and acquisition, to the complex and situated nature of how languages are produced and consumed, can grow into confident and powerful users of language.

Mastery of SAE is associated with prescriptive standards such as those named in this section of the Common Core; however, to understand such prescriptive standards as uncomplicated would reflect a limited understanding of the intersections of language, learning, and culture. This reveals a key limitation of prescriptive standards, which are based on one community's definitions of knowledge and skills. While skills associated with SAE can provide students access to academic opportunity, the cultural and historical origins of SAE and the fact that decisions about "official" language norms and rules are socially constructed are concealed in instruction that does not explicitly expose them. That is, if instruction based on standards does not refer to the socially constructed nature of the rules on which standards are based, then students will have an incomplete understanding of how language works. Learning language as primarily involving adherence to a set of rules restricts how language might be imagined differently, and likewise limits possible uses of language. Further, for students whose home and community language practices do not mirror classroom-based practices, an unexamined focus on academic language can reinforce alienation from school. Prescriptive standards offer a snapshot of academic English, as well as transparent criteria for assessing teaching and learning. They can facilitate lesson planning and contribute to the implementation of coherent, cohesive curriculum. On the other hand, curriculum based on unexamined prescriptive standards can leave little room for imagination or diversity of thought.

Prescriptive standards can be a useful way of organizing skills and knowledge. Because they reflect received knowledge, their analysis can offer a linguistic window into spaces of power and privilege; however, they can also reinforce mechanisms of exclusion, especially when linked with standardized assessments. Limitations of prescriptive standards can be mitigated by centering learners, seeing them as already effective participants in language communities, and building on what they know and are able to do.

This does not imply that instructional practices associated with prescriptive standards are always rote, teacher-centered, and coupled with tedious assessments. Creative, student-centered pedagogies and authentic assessments can address a range of instructional aims, including those related to SAE. Instruction in which students read, write, speak, and listen for purposes that are meaningful to them and their communities can involve complex applications of language that are tailored for various audiences and assessed in multiple contexts.

Aspirational standards, as the term implies, refer to an ideal – a condition toward which we strive through continuous improvement. On a large scale, an aspirational standard might be that *schools will provide equal opportunities for all learners to reach their potential*. Progress has been made, as demonstrated by policies addressing special education and English language learners, but much remains to be done. The ideal of *justice* is a standard toward which educators must always aim, even knowing that the goal will remain on the horizon. A receding horizon illustrates the concept of an aspirational standard. As we approach the horizon, nearby images come into focus, and previously unseen phenomena appear in the distance.

Aspirational standards can be found throughout the field, and have common characteristics. They are generally applicable to a wide range of age and ability levels, and are open ended, which complicates their assessment. NCTE and the International Reading Association (IRA), for example, collaborated in the development of 12 standards that span pre-Kindergarten through grade 12. The standards are student-centered, broad, and inclusive, as can be seen in this excerpt:

9. Students develop an understanding of and *respect for diversity* (all emphasis mine) in language use, patterns, and dialects across cultures, ethnic groups, geographic regions, and social roles.

10. Students whose first language is not English make use of their first language to *develop competency* in the English language arts and to develop understanding of content across the curriculum.

11. Students participate as knowledgeable, *reflective, creative, and critical* members of a variety of literacy communities.

12. Students use spoken, written, and visual language to accomplish their own purposes (e.g., for learning, *enjoyment*, persuasion, and the exchange of information).

The Common Core Standards (CCS) also provide some standards that are more aspirational than prescriptive. The CCS literacy standard addressing writing for grades 11 and 12 states that students will "Write informative/explanatory texts to examine and convey complex ideas, concepts, and information clearly and accurately through the effective selection, organization, and analysis of content." This, I would argue, is a standard I continue to aspire to, a standard I am seeking to reach even as I am writing this book. The subcomponents are a bit more detailed, but not prescriptive.

CCSS.ELA-LITERACY.W.11-12.2.A

Introduce a topic; organize complex ideas, concepts, and information so that each new element builds on that which precedes it to create a unified whole; include formatting (e.g., headings), graphics (e.g., figures, tables), and multimedia when useful to aiding comprehension.

CCSS.ELA-LITERACY.W.11-12.2.B

Develop the topic thoroughly by selecting the most significant and relevant facts, extended definitions, concrete details, quotations, or other information and examples appropriate to the audience's knowledge of the topic.

According to the subcomponents, student writers are perceived to be able to determine how to aid reader comprehension, and to have the wherewithal to select pertinent details germane to topics and audiences. Aspirational standards are beneficial in that they promote authentic application and ongoing growth. Their expansiveness and complexity complicates assessment because progress toward aspirational standards can be difficult to quantify and rank. This is illustrated in the italicized terms in the excerpt from the NCTE standards 9, 10, 11, and 12. These concepts are particularly challenging to assess, even more so in a standardized format.

Like opportunity-to-learn standards, aspirational standards tend to portray students and teachers as decision-makers in the learning process. In public schools today, standards-based curricula dominate instruction and assessment. Ranging from very broad (Students will be able to read, write, speak, and listen for information and understanding) to specific (Students will use an ellipsis to indicate a break), standards can be tools for dominance or levers for learning. Despite various origins and authorial agencies, standards are often presented as authoritative, agreed-upon disciplinary pillars of knowledge and skills. However, as experts in content and pedagogy, teachers must critically examine standards and determine how students can engage with them in authentic and meaningful ways.

Multicultural Education

In the current educational context, which is dominated by standards-based decision-making, it can be hard to imagine an alternative orientation toward instructional planning. Multiculturalism offers such an orientation. The National Association for Multicultural Education (NAME), while acknowledging that competing and parallel definitions exist, defines "multicultural education" as a philosophical concept, a process, and an approach grounded in critical advocacy. Philosophically, multicultural education includes ideals such as "freedom, justice, equality, equity, and human dignity." Multiculturalism takes a systemic perspective, explicitly recognizing:

> ...the role schools can play in developing the attitudes and values necessary for a democratic society. It values cultural differences and affirms the pluralism that students, their communities, and teachers reflect. It challenges all forms of discrimination in schools and society through the promotion of democratic principles of social justice.

As a process, multicultural education puts these beliefs into action with curricula and instruction that reflects the philosophy. Significantly, multiculturalism explicitly recognizes how roles of students and teachers influence education, thus encouraging investigation of familiar contexts. Multicultural curricula encourage students and teachers to identify and challenge injustice in schools and beyond. Multiculturalism centers on the lived experiences of students, diverse ways of thinking, and critical analysis of systems of power and oppression in local and global contexts.

On the surface, multiculturalism may seem incompatible with standards-based instruction; however, Sleeter elaborates on this perception, explaining the impact of implementation and, therefore, the significance of the role of teachers. Sleeter notes that:

…standards and multicultural education are not compatible when standards cause educators to shift attention away from what students know and care about based on their lives … [and] when standards structure curriculum around perspectives that best fit those of middle-class Americans of European descent.

Sleeter draws attention to the role of teachers as educational visionaries who can interpret and implement standards in ways that empower students and value their cultures. Implemented wisely, standards can emphasize how curricular bias can be a barrier to students from historically marginalized populations. However, she also acknowledges how assessments related to standards can restrict academic freedom and impede educational opportunities. A critical pedagogical approach, in which contexts are continually examined, supports teachers in addressing standards in ways that are compatible with multiculturalism.

An example of a critical approach in practice involves the **equity literacy framework** (Gorski), which "refers to the knowledge and skills that enable us to recognize, respond to, and redress conditions that deny some students access to educational and other opportunities enjoyed by their peers." The equity literacy framework focuses on teachers' development of skills, as well as cultural competence, to support all students. In the framework, Gorski identifies four competencies related to equity literacy:

1. Ability to recognize biases and inequities, including subtle biases and inequities
2. Ability to respond to biases and inequities in the immediate term
3. Ability to redress biases and inequities in the long term
4. Ability to create and sustain a bias-free and equitable learning environment

In the framework, each of these skills is expanded to reveal actions related to equity-oriented perspectives. To demonstrate the ability to "redress biases and inequities in the long term," for example, teachers might

- advocate against inequitable school practices, such as racially or economically biased tracking, and advocate for equitable school practices;
- never confuse celebrating diversity with equity, such as by responding to racial conflict with cultural celebrations; and
- teach, in relevant and age-appropriate ways, about issues like sexism, poverty, and homophobia.

The equity literacy framework makes multicultural principles concrete, merging critical theory and practice. Similarly, sj Miller's Queer Literacy Framework encourages teachers to support youth in reimagining language, texts, and identities. Originating from the understanding "that students' identities are affected by teachers' beliefs and perceptions of adolescence/ts," (39) the framework is intended to encourage teachers to "remain open to evolving understandings of (a)gender and (a)sexuality," with the goal of transforming schools and society toward justice.

These are just two examples of how pedagogical frameworks can work within existing epistemologies to influence classroom practice. Theory and practice continuously intersect, each informing the other, and each influenced by beliefs about roles of students and teachers.

From Culturally Relevant to Culturally Sustaining Pedagogies

Drawing on Ladson-Billings' theory of **culturally relevant pedagogy**, culturally responsive education systems work at the intersection of people, practices, and policies. Culturally responsive educators demonstrate the capacity to "learn from and relate respectfully with people of your own culture as well as those from other cultures." Built on principles of content integration, equity pedagogy, school culture, prejudice reduction, and knowledge construction, culturally responsive pedagogies balance high expectations with student-centered instruction, and explicitly address issues of power and freedom in the classroom. Relationships are perceived as essential to effective instruction, and teachers are meant to be advocates for learners and their families. Recently, however, Paris argued that culturally relevant pedagogies, while important, do not go far enough in challenging a monocultural and monolingual orientation toward education. Paris claims that, "to perpetuate and foster – to sustain – linguistic, literate, and cultural pluralism as part of the democratic project of schooling," (93) **culturally sustaining pedagogies** are necessary. Culturally sustaining pedagogies aim to disrupt policies that maintain systems of oppression by embracing cultural pluralism and cultural equality. Moving from tolerance of multicultural perspectives within a dominant framework to *cultivation* of a pluralistic orientation may seem subtle, but it is significant. Cultural responsiveness can be represented by initiatives such as Black History Month or electives focused on Indigenous literature. Both of these ventures are well-intentioned, but fail to de-center dominant paradigms. In fact, their marginalized nature re-instantiates White, Western perspectives. A culturally sustaining approach, on the other hand, begins with questions about whose literature counts, and why. The roles of teachers and students are decision-makers, creators of curriculum that reflects cultural diversity and that aims to reveal and interrupt inequities.

Summary

Beliefs about the roles of teachers and learners have profound effects on the classroom experiences, and thus on how students and teachers engage with language and texts. Policies, enacted through assessments and frameworks, reflect epistemologies that affect how teachers and learners interact with one another, and with content. And all these facets are expressed through language, the discipline central to English classrooms. The intersections discussed in this chapter are complex, and require ongoing critical examination, as theories and practices are continually questioned. A just society is an aspiration, and education, as an aspirational endeavor, depends on how teachers perceive their roles, and how they perceive the roles of students.

Extension Questions

1. Assumptions are deeply held, and often unexamined, beliefs. Assumptions are shaped by experiences and they influence our actions by shaping how we imagine the way things "ought to be." Think about the assumptions you have about classrooms and schools, and identify one to examine, using Table 2.1 as an example.
2. Select an example of a prescriptive standard related to English. It can be from a professional organization, a state or federal policy initiative, or from a a different source. Explain the strengths and weaknesses of the standard, and interpret how the roles of teachers and students are revealed in the standard.
3. Select an example of an aspirational standard related to English. What beliefs about teachers, learning, and schools can be inferred? How might achievement in relation to the standards be assessed?
4. Research indicates that "As teachers increase their own personal teaching efficacy – the belief in themselves that they are effective teachers and can produce desired student outcomes – they often become more effective teachers because they are less concerned about the demands of teacher tasks and more likely to adopt innovative approaches that support diverse learning needs" (Hartlep, McCubbins, Hansen, Banicki, and Morgan, 3). Do you agree or disagree with this contention? What experiences in your own background connect with this claim?

TABLE 2.1 Examining Beliefs

Assumption	Source	Effect	Alternative perspective	Related scholarly literature
Homework is related to academic achievement	In elementary, middle school, and high school, students who completed homework experienced academic success.	As a teacher, I assigned homework and rewarded its completion.	Homework reinscribes privilege, since some learners have access to resources that enable them to complete homework, while others do not.	Stanford research shows pitfalls of homework https://news.stanford.edu/2014/03/10/too-much-hom ework-031014/ Nonacademic Effects of Homework in Privileged, High-Performing High Schools www.tandfonline.com/doi/abs/10.1080/00220973.2012.745469

5. English education has a long, distinguished history, much of which is related to canons of literature. Consider how texts reflect beliefs about students and teachers, and discuss how classroom uses of texts can affect learning experiences.

Works Cited

Cajete, Gregory. *Spirit of the Game: An Indigenous Wellspring*. Durango, CO: Kivaki Press, 2004.

Common Core State Standards Initiative. *Conventions of Standard English*, 2017. www.cor estandards.org/ELA-Literacy/.

Freire, Paulo. *Pedagogy of the Oppressed*. New York, NY: Herder & Herder, 1970.

Gorski, Paul C. *Reaching and Teaching Students in Poverty: Strategies for Erasing the Opportunity Gap*. New York, NY: Teachers College Press, 2014. Excerpted: www.edchange. org/handouts/Equity-Literacy-Introduction.pdf.

Hartlep, Nicholas D., Sara McCubbins, Christopher M. Hansen, Guy J. Banicki and Grant B. Morgan. (2014) *What Makes a Star Teacher? Examining the Dispositions of PK12 Urban Teachers in Chicago*. Illinois State University Department of Educational Administration and Foundations. http://works.bepress.com/nicholas_hartlep/10/

Hillocks, George Jr. "Middle and High School Composition." In *Research on Composition: Multiple Perspectives on Two Decades of Change* (Peter Smagorinsky, Editor.). New York, NY: Teachers College Press, pp. 48–77, 2005.

Ladson-Billings, Gloria. "Toward a Theory of Culturally Relevant Pedagogy." *American Educational Research Journal*, vol. 32, no. 3, pp. 465–491, Autumn 1995.

Langer, Judith A. and Arthur N. Applebee. *How Writing Shapes Thinking: A Study of Teaching and Learning*. Urbana, IL: National Council of Teachers of English, 1987.

Lyiscott, Jamila. "Racial Identity and Liberation Literacies in the Classroom." *English Journal*, vol. 106, no. 4, pp. 47–53, March 2017.

NCTE. *Professional Knowledge for the Teaching of Writing*. Urbana, IL: National Council of Teachers of English, February 2016.

NCTE Executive Committee. *Opportunity-to-Learn Standards, Statement of Principles*. National Council of Teachers of English, 1996. www2.ncte.org/statement/opptolea rnstandards/.

NCTE Executive Committee, and the IRA Board of Directors. *Standards for the English Language Arts*. Urbana, IL: National Council of Teachers of English, and the International Reading Association, 1996.

Ng, Wan, Howard Nicholas, and Alan Williams. "School Experience Influences on Pre-Service Teachers' Evolving Beliefs about Effective Teaching." *Teaching and Teacher Education*, vol. 26, no. 2, pp. 278–289, February 2010.

Miller, sj. "A Queer Literacy Framework Promoting (A)Gender and (A)Sexuality Self-Determination and Justice." *English Journal*, vol. 104, no. 5, pp. 37–44, May 2015.

Mueller, Jon. *Authentic Assessment Toolbox*. 2016. http://jfmueller.faculty.noctrl.edu/tool box/standardtypes.htm.

Oates, Scott F. "Literacy as Everyday Practice." In *Constructions of Literacy: Studies of Teaching and Learning In and Out of Secondary Schools* (Elizabeth B. Moje and David G. O'Brien, Editors.) Mahwah, NJ: Erlbaum, pp. 213–237, 2001.

Paris, Django. "Culturally Sustaining Pedagogy: A Needed Change in Stance, Terminology, and Practice." *Educational Researcher*, vol. 41, no. 3, pp. 93–97, April 2012. http://web.stanford.edu/class/linguist159/restricted/readings/Paris2012.pdf.

Patel, Leigh. *Decolonizing Educational Research: From Ownership to Answerability*. Abingdon, UK: Routledge, 2015.

Reigeluth, Charles M. "Educational Standards: To Standardize or to Customize Learning?" *Phi Delta Kappan*, vol. 79, no. 3, pp. 202–206, 1997. www.jstor.org/stable/pdf/20405991.pdf?refreqid=excelsior%3A24bbec8c7e348ec86f0771d6f8d85204.

Rosen, Charles. *The Romantic Generation*. Cambridge, MA: Harvard University Press, 1995.

Sleeter, Christine E. "Are Standards and Multicultural Education Compatible?" *ASCD Express*, vol. 6, no. 15, 2011. www.ascd.org/ascd-express/vol6/615-sleeter.aspx.

The English Spelling Society. *FAQs*. http://spellingsociety.org/faqs.

The English Spelling Society. *Press Release – Wednesday 20th April, 2016*. http://spellingsociety.org/press-release-wednesday-20th-april-2016_sc5.

The National Association for Multicultural Education. *Definitions of Multicultural Education*. www.nameorg.org/definitions_of_multicultural_e.php.

Thiong'o, Ngũgĩ wa. *Decolonising the Mind: The Politics of Language in African Literature*. London, UK: Heinemann Educational Books, 1986.

Tuck, Eve K. and Wayne Yang. "Decolonization is Not a Metaphor." *Decolonization: Indigeneity, Education, & Society*, vol. 1, no 1, pp. 1–40, 2012.

Wertheim, Cheruta and Yona Leyser. "Efficacy Beliefs, Background Variables, and Differentiated Instruction of Israeli Prospective Teachers." *The Journal of Educational Research*, vol. 96, no. 1, pp. 54–63, September–October 2002.

3

CURRICULUM IN ENGLISH CLASSROOMS

Who Should Decide?

"I am not reading anything from this book." Michelle's voice was calm and measured, but her manner was intense, reflecting poise beyond what would be typical of a 16 year old.

Maureen, stunned by this uncharacteristic defiance from a student she knew well, struggled to gather her thoughts and craft a coherent response. It was the first week of school and only her second meeting with this 11th grade class, but Michelle had been one of her best students last year, in the elective Creative Writing course. She took a deep breath and decided to try to defuse the tension with a direct question, and a bit of humor.

"Michelle, what's wrong with this book? I know it weighs a ton, but that's why I gave you a copy to keep at home, so you don't have to carry it to class every day."

Michelle didn't return Maureen's smile. "You can add this one to the class set, Miss Gallagher" she replied, gesturing toward the bookshelves under the window. "I won't be needing it."

"Michelle, can you at least explain why you're upset, so I can try to address your concerns," Maureen tried again. "Any book this size is bound to have something for everyone!"

Once more, the joke fell flat. Michelle blinked slowly and met Maureen's gaze. "This book has nothing for me. According to this book, I don't even exist! Native Americans disappeared in 1620!"

She reached over and flipped the anthology open to the Table of Contents. "Find a reference to Native American literature after Unit One. Go ahead and try! Why should I read a book that thinks I exist only in history?"

"Just a second, Michelle, a book is more than a Table of Contents. Did you look at the introduction to the unit? It explicitly addresses the fact that Native American literature is alive and well. In fact, it calls Native American literature 'our country's first literature.'" That particular line had stayed with Maureen, who had been impressed by the cultural awareness reflected in the introductory passage. Since about 20% of her student population included Native American students, she had read that section of the anthology carefully – and had never anticipated this kind of reaction, especially from a high-achieving student like Michelle.

"Okay, Miss Gallagher, if Native American literature is so relevant, why does it end on page 109 of a book that is 1,378 pages long?" She flipped angrily through the first few

pages. "Listen to some of the authors in the last unit, War Abroad and Conflict at Home*: Bernard Malamud, John Steinbeck, Joan Didion, Tim O'Brien, Yusef Komunyakaa, Tran Thi Nga, Denise Levertov, Martin Luther King, Nikki Giovanni, Gary Soto, Pat Mora, Garrett Hongo, Amy Tan, Sandra Cisneros. I guess Native American authors don't have anything to say about 'conflict at home', right?" She slammed the book closed and took a deep breath, then looked up at Maureen. "I want to do well in this class, Miss Gallagher. But I will not read anything in this book."*

Broadly defined, *curriculum* encompasses everything that teachers teach and students learn in school. Curriculum includes what is written in instructional plans, what is taught, what is learned, and what is tested. This understanding of curriculum includes content, skills, and behaviors that are cultivated, both intentionally and unintentionally. For example, a teacher who is trying to instill appreciation of classical literature might inadvertently impart the notion that literature of value is primarily created by White, English-speaking men who followed Western traditions of narrative structure. Even though that is likely not part of the official curriculum, it is experienced by students as part of what has been labeled the "hidden curriculum."

This chapter will discuss how components of curriculum are perceived and enacted by teachers and students in English classrooms. Concepts and key terms such as the written, delivered, and received curriculum will be described, and distinctions among how curriculum is taught, learned, and tested will be explored. Additionally discussed will be issues such as the hidden curriculum and its relationship to cultural capital and how standards-based and multicultural education manifest themselves in classroom activities. This chapter will also consider the "null" curriculum – in other words, what it left out of formal instructional contexts, as well as horizontal and vertical curriculum alignment.

The overarching question about curriculum that frames this chapter is revealed in the title: *who decides?* Furthermore, the consequences of curricular decisions can be analyzed by questioning *who benefits* and *who loses?* Because language is never neutral, language instruction can never be neutral. Although curriculum is often perceived by teachers and students as prescribed, in reality it is shaped by policy-makers, textbook authors/editors and publishers, authorities in the discipline, and classroom teachers. This chapter will unpack the beliefs and assumptions introduced in previous chapters in order to explore how the perspectives of various **stakeholders** influence the development of curriculum. These perspectives will be juxtaposed with how curriculum is perceived and delivered from a critical theoretical standpoint. The chapter will conclude with a series of guiding questions designed to facilitate analysis of curriculum to which readers have been exposed.

As briefly addressed in Chapter 2, curriculum is multidimensional, involving a range of stakeholders that shape its development and delivery. As a **social construction**, curriculum is produced by discourse and affected by culture. Curriculum theorist Apple explained:

> Education is deeply implicated in the politics of culture. The curriculum is never a neutral assemblage of knowledge, somehow appearing in the texts and classrooms of a nation. It is always part of a *selective tradition*, someone's selection, some group's vision of legitimate knowledge. It is produced out of the cultural, political, and economic conflicts, tensions, and compromises that organise and disorganise a people. (1)

Curricular decisions reflect how power in society is distributed unequally; some stakeholders have greater influence on decisions related to curriculum than others. Furthermore, because curriculum is multidimensional effects of decisions vary. The complexity of its origins and diversity of its implementation makes curriculum impacts difficult to determine. However, its broad strokes and material outcomes are discernible. It may be helpful to imagine curriculum as an octopus. As a cephalopod, curriculum's tentacles can extend to gather and distribute information. On the surface, tentacles and suction cups can seem to move independently, even in opposite directions at times. Imagine these tentacles as various approaches to curriculum, which emerge from one pluralistic society but touch learners in various ways. At their ends, they may appear disconnected, and there is even evidence that they move independently. However, at the source they are unified – a characteristic that is revealed when the octopus engages muscles in separate tentacles to move in a particular direction. Movements of individual tentacles may seem arbitrary, but the organism's locomotion is coordinated.

This metaphor is not meant to imply that a central set of machinations control the evolution of curriculum. However, it illustrates how seemingly disparate understandings and implementations of curriculum can have far-reaching effects on every aspect of education. Curriculum, sometimes defined as everything that teachers teach and students learn, has been shown to shape, and be shaped by, **social class**. As such, it has profound effects on the lives and life chances of learners. In the next section, connections among social class, schooling, and curriculum with be discussed, and the **"hidden curriculum"** will be further explored.

Schooling and Social Class

Anyone who has visited a range of schools has noted sometimes profound differences between and among them. Sometimes differences are related to a community's choices, such as offering students opportunities to participate in marching band instead of orchestra, or lacrosse rather than basketball. Often, however, differences reflect disparities that result in inequitable access to educational opportunities. Some schools, for example, offer numerous college-level courses and other rich academic experiences that improve students' ability to succeed in post-secondary settings. Other schools offer few, or no, college-level courses, and little access to challenging instructional experiences. To investigate how such differences manifest from a sociological perspective, educational researcher Jean Anyon conducted a study of elementary schools serving students from groups categorized as follows: working class, middle class, affluent professional, and executive elite. Consistent with a capacious understanding of curriculum, Anyon considered instruction and evaluation practices and analyzed how these practices correspond to skills and traits associated with social class. The idea that schools prepare children for work that aligns with their respective social class has been deliberated for decades by prominent scholars:

> Bowles and Gintis, for example, have argued that students in different social-class backgrounds are rewarded for classroom behaviors that correspond to personality traits allegedly rewarded in the different occupational strata—the working classes for docility and obedience, the managerial classes for initiative and personal assertiveness. Basil Bernstein, Pierre Bourdieu, and Michael W. Apple focusing on school knowledge, have argued that knowledge and skills leading to social power and regard (medical, legal, managerial) are made available to the advantaged social groups but are withheld from the working classes to whom a more "practical" curriculum is offered (manual skills, clerical knowledge). (67)

Although much attention had been paid to the idea that schools reinforce social class, Anyon's study provided empirical evidence supporting theoretical claims. Over the course of an academic year, her study looked at coursework, materials, assessments, and student-teacher interactions in 5th-grade classrooms. In terms of school and community context, Anyon's findings indicated that higher social class was associated with more and better classroom materials and school equipment; increased support for teacher planning and professional development; higher levels of educational attainment by administrators, teachers, and parents; stricter and more demanding academic requirements; and higher expectations for student achievement.

Anyon also found that instruction in working-class schools focused on compliance and following procedures. In English language arts, for example, students were presented with rules of grammar and instructed to follow them with neither explanation nor elaboration. Instruction in middle-class schools emphasized obtaining the right answer, but did offer opportunities for students to exercise choice. Language arts instruction focused on speaking and writing properly, selecting the "right" answers, and understanding the reasons behind the correct choices. In affluent professional schools, teachers stressed individual thought, expressiveness, elaboration of ideas, and choice. In contrast to the working-class and middle-class schools, English language arts instruction minimized grammar and focused on creative writing often based on authentic experiences. Curriculum experiences in the executive elite school emphasized analytical, intellectual work demonstrated through research and projects involving problem-solving. Academic excellence was a high priority. English language arts work required students to lead instructional activities in which they were assessed on criteria such as presentation, communication, and class control. In addition, knowledge is perceived differently in each setting. In working-class schools, teachers are perceived as the sole sources of knowledge and authority. In middle-class schools, books are perceived as repositories of knowledge, and in executive elite schools, students are perceived as a source of knowledge. These differing perceptions influence students' trust in their own literacy practices, and in their own ideas. All these experiences, Anyon concluded, demonstrate that the "hidden curriculum" of school work sets children up to remain within their social class and thus perpetuates the maintenance of the status quo and the gap between rich and poor. (89–90).

Social Class and the Hidden Curriculum

Because the practices Anyon identified were customary within each school, they were not obvious to stakeholders. In essence, these practices simply represented school culture as "the way things are done around here." School culture is comprised of all aspects of curriculum, including what Fenwick English (16) defines as the "hidden curriculum":

> This curriculum is the one rarely discussed in schools. It is not even recognized by many educators who work in them. The hidden curriculum is the one that is taught without formal recognition. For example, American children are taught to be "neat and clean," "on time," and "respectful" to teachers. These "lessons" are rarely contained within formal curricula. But they are powerful conventions and norms that are at work in schools nonetheless.
>
> The hidden curriculum contains "structured silences" (Aronowitz & Giroux) that embody expectations and presuppositions about social conduct that often place disadvantaged students "at risk" in schools and work against them by being ignorant of the inherent cultural biases that are embedded in school rules.

In his explanation of the "hidden curriculum," English makes two ideas clear. First, the hidden curriculum *exists*; its effects are powerful and ubiquitous. And second, without explicit attention, i.e., a critical approach to the assumptions that produce the hidden curriculum, it remains invisible and, thus, unexamined. It is, in fact, the unexamined (and therefore veiled) nature of the hidden curriculum that makes it potentially problematic for students. If, in fact, our education system values behaviors that exemplify neatness and respect, then we should not hesitate to openly teach and assess these behaviors.

Cultural norms, however, seem natural and normal to those who are cultural natives, so problems arise when what the school culture defines as a "respectful" behavior differs from the student's home culture. For example, teachers in the

United States generally expect students to make eye contact in order to show respect and indicate that they are paying attention. Not all cultures would perceive student-teacher eye contact as respectful; in fact, it might even be identified as defiant. It is easy to imagine how such a cultural dissonance might arise in schools, as well as how a lack of familiarity with the hidden curricula of schooling might disadvantage certain students. While the hidden curriculum can exacerbate inequities, educators who are reflective about their pedagogies and the cultural norms of schooling can help students learn to navigate cultural differences by revealing and explicating the hidden curriculum.

A related aspect of the hidden curriculum involves **cultural capital**. In and of themselves, cultural norms are not associated with value or power. Music produced by a songbird is equivalent to a symphony. However, as the example shows, society ascribes various values to products, processes, and norms. Despite similar linguistic complexity, Shakespearean sonnets are associated with greater cultural capital than hip hop. Sociologist Pierre Bourdieu described these values as "cultural capital." He noted that such values are influenced by everyday practices of ordinary people, as well as exercises of political power. Because of these forces, values associated with cultural capital change over time, and they influence decisions about curriculum.

This discussion of social class, the hidden curriculum, and cultural capital sets the stage for the significance of analyzing how curricular decisions are made. Understanding the implications of curriculum on the lives of learners emphasizes the importance of embracing a critical perspective regarding what is taught, how it is taught (including the quality of facilities and resources available to teachers and students), what is learned, and how it is assessed. The next sections will discuss how the explicit curriculum is delivered and received.

Types of Curriculum

From the broad definition of curriculum as everything that students learn and teachers teach can be derived narrower categories, such as the **explicit** or **formal curriculum**. As the term implies, the explicit curriculum is the formal, stated curriculum found in textbooks, curriculum guides, and standards. Publicly recognized by the school as its academic focus, the explicit curriculum is sometimes referred to as the **written curriculum**. This is the most common conception of curriculum, and is a good starting point for thinking about how curricular decisions are made.

Because it is formal, and often published, the explicit curriculum is generally perceived to be definitive; its existence can conceal other ways that curricula are produced and consumed. This monolithic perception of curriculum can also obscure the decision-making processes that shape curricula. Without critical examination of content and skills presented, curriculum guides, standards, and textbooks can give the impression that information is provided by an omniscient, anonymous expert. Unquestioned acceptance of an explicit curriculum leaves its orientation opaque, hiding the fact that people, organizations, and governing bodies *decide* what is included, how information is organized, and how content and skills are assessed. Such decisions also determine what is left out.

Time is a key consideration in curricular decisions. Because time is limited, some content and skills must be left out. Some materials are omitted entirely, thus becoming part of the **null curriculum** – what schools do not teach. The null curriculum might consist of content, such as mythology or evolution; skills, such as creative writing or public speaking; or disciplines, such as ethnic studies. The null curriculum can also reflect what is omitted from a particular worldview. For example, the traditional canon of literature was composed almost exclusively of authors who were White, male, and from Western literary traditions. The null curriculum matters because what is included, or excluded, from school experiences signifies what is valid and valued. Similar to the hidden curriculum, the null curriculum sends messages about what knowledge and skills are important, acceptable, and worth learning. Outside of classroom instruction, the null curriculum intersects with the **extra curriculum**, which includes activities that are connected to, sanctioned by, and usually organized within, schools, but do not confer credit. Extracurricular activities, though marginalized in relation to the explicit curriculum, can signal cultural capital. It can be informative to explore how resources are allocated for various activities, and how extracurricular events garner attention from students, teachers, and community members. Although the extra curriculum tends to be student centered, not all student interests are encompassed by extracurricular activities. Different conceptions of cultural capital are revealed in what is included in, and left out of, all categories of school curricula.

A wide range of stakeholders are involved in decisions about explicit curricula, and many resources contribute to their development. Textbooks are expensive to produce; therefore, it is more efficient to create new editions that begin by replicating existing books. Without critical examination, this can reproduce knowledge associated with greater cultural capital. Textbooks are also affected by policies related to their adoption. For example, the Texas Board of Education adopts textbooks for all public schools in the state, while in New York, local school boards decide on textbooks. Therefore, it is much more lucrative for publishers to consult closely with policymakers in Texas, since meeting their needs can result in sales that dwarf a purchase made by a school district in New York State. It makes sense, then, for publishers to produce textbooks for states like Texas, and then revise them to accommodate states like New York. These conditions allow decision-making power to be unequally distributed.

In addition to publishers, other sources of written curriculum include standards, which were discussed in depth in Chapter 2, as well as professional organizations, state agencies, regional consortia, and local schools. Professional organizations often draw on the work of practicing teachers, building on position statements in order to develop model lesson plans. State agencies may lead groups of teachers in the development of curriculum guides, and even in the development and scoring of large-scale assessments. While these endeavors can empower teachers and bring decision-making closer to the classroom, it is important to investigate which stakeholders are involved, the levels of involvement to which they have access, how their participation is supported, and the types of decisions afforded to various stakeholder groups. For example, being invited to write multiple choice questions for assessments addressing prescribed standards is different from being involved in the development of the standards, themselves. Consideration of such decisions leads to a discussion of the how curriculum is delivered and received, specifically how content and skills are taught, learned, and tested.

Curriculum Enacted

The shift from curriculum as a written product to an instructional process occurs when curriculum is implemented. Curriculum, when it is put into practice with learners, is called the **delivered curriculum**. As with any activity that is mediated by humans, the delivered curriculum is subject to interpretation, negotiation, and modification. Even when curriculum includes **scripted lessons** that direct teachers to use exact verbiage provided, the execution of instruction can vary with tone, inflections, gestures, and facial expressions. Less specific forms of curriculum are even more permeable to changes related to delivery. Imagine, for example, the infinite interpretations of a curriculum guide that includes lists of required (or recommended) literature, concepts, and skills. A teacher charged to teach *Romeo and Juliet* could approach the task in innumerable ways. In addition to the plot, she might focus on language and literary devices, on characterization and the sociological implications of character development and portrayal, on the Elizabethan age and the architecture and logistics of the Globe Theater, on dramatic terms and elements, or on the themes and conflicts around youth, age, and wisdom. Many teachers would integrate a combination of these – all of which would be addressed in conjunction with an understanding of the plot.

Differences between the explicit curriculum and the delivered curriculum offer opportunities for teachers to exercise professional judgment and develop their pedagogical repertoire. Even the strictest written curriculum guides leave space for choice, and critical educators can often shift the lens on texts, encouraging learners to consider alternative perspectives by asking how curricular decisions are made, and who benefits and who loses from these decisions.

Thinking about encounters between the delivered curriculum and intended learners raises the concept of the **received curriculum**. This concept is illustrated in a comic called Tiger, created by Bud Blake, which centers on a conversation between two young people and a dog, Stripe. In the first frame, one tells his friend, "I taught Stripe to whistle." In the second frame, the friend, nose to nose with Stripe, replies, "I don't hear him whistling." In the third and final frame, the youth defends himself, explaining, "I said I taught him. I didn't say he learned it." This comic illustrates a distinction that is often unnoticed: regardless of how well or relentlessly teachers teach, our success depends on learners. They need the capacity and motivation to engage with instruction in ways that influence their performance. Fortunately, despite the significance of out-of-school factors, teachers can develop both capacity and motivation in learners. First, such development must be recognized as part of the role of teachers. And second, teachers must understand the importance of correspondence between the delivered and received curricula. This correspondence boils down to two questions: 1) What do I want students to learn? and 2) How will I know they have learned it? As these questions reveal, the delivered curriculum corresponds to what is taught and the received curriculum to what is learned. A third consideration, hinted at in question 2, involves assessment. That is, analysis of curriculum implementation should examine what is taught, what is learned, and what is tested.

Correspondence among what is taught, what is learned, and what is tested is one aspect of curriculum integrity. Such correspondence can be specific to a lesson, a unit, or a year-long plan of study. The idea of curriculum integrity can be extended, however, beyond individual classrooms and academic years. This concept, which is important because student experiences of curriculum transcend classrooms and grade levels, is called curriculum alignment. Curriculum alignment is mapped along two axes: horizontal and vertical. **Horizontal alignment** considers what is taught and learned in the same grade level in different classrooms. For example, do all 9th-grade English classes identify the features of a Shakespearean sonnet? **Vertical alignment** examines what is taught and learned from one grade level to the next. In terms of content and skills, a curriculum characterized by good vertical alignment would scaffold activities from one year to the next. For example, eighth graders may focus on persuasive essays and preparation for the more complex argumentative essays which are often taught in grade 9. Areas of omission or duplication in vertical alignment can have negative consequences for learners. Gaps in vertical alignment can result in students lacking access to knowledge and skills that they are expected to have. This can set them up for failure, preventing them from earning credits or credentials. Duplication in vertical alignment, especially when content is not meaningful for students, can contribute to their boredom and alienation from school. **Curriculum mapping** can reveal areas of omission and repetition. Curriculum mapping brings teachers together to compare knowledge and skills. Well-crafted curriculum mapping activities will compare written curriculum, delivered curriculum, and received curriculum (through student assessments and/or interviews). The map, or visual representation of these curricula, will show where gaps and repetition exist. Rich mapping undertakings will also consider how the null and extra-curriculum relate to the values of the community and the lives of learners. This answerability to learners is essential; without it schools can have an aligned curriculum in which the implicit, or unwritten, curriculum undermines the intent of the written curriculum. For example, if students are assigned to read literature that they don't relate to, they learn to loathe reading. If reading is repeatedly associated with failure, they learn that their literacy skills are deficient. Both experiences contribute to an **implicit** or **informal curriculum** that works against stated purposes. Students are meant to learn to read; instead, they learn to hate reading, and that they are bad readers.

Accountability and Answerability

Decisions about curriculum are made by many stakeholders who have various interests. Political leaders have a stake in ensuring that they and their parties remain in power. Public agencies intend to serve what they perceive as the common good. Community and cultural organizations aim to satisfy their constituents. Professional associations function in the political arena and seek to grow the influence and status of their organization and its members. Purveyors of curriculum seek to make a profit. Parents center their children's present well-being and future success. In an ideal society, these objectives would align, and like the octopus performing jet propulsion, all the tentacles would aim in the same direction, supporting coordinated progress toward a shared goal. However, in a pluralistic society where dissent is encouraged and power relations can be challenged, stakeholders' aspirations differ. Because the purposes of curricula are constructed around the needs of learners, it can be difficult to see how stakeholders' interests vary. One way to get a clear picture of these interests is to look through the lenses of **accountability** and **answerability**. As a reminder, in Chapter 1 accountability was defined as having three parts: meeting expectations, taking responsibility, and reporting transparently. These general principles are helpful, but they can also obscure the importance of answerability. That is, *to whom* are educators accountable? Who or what entities decide on expectations, determine where responsibilities lie and establish reporting criteria? The shift in thinking from accountability to answerability is significant; it changes educational goals. Accountability is based on static, dominant, and predetermined outcomes, measured against norms and values likely to support existing power relations. A focus on accountability centers on institutions, in which people will succeed or fail in relation to decisions made without their input. Answerability resets that center, focusing on the lives, aspirations, needs, and desires of learners, their families, and their communities. Schools and curricula, from the standpoint of answerability, should first respond to the stakeholders most affected by decisions: students. Discussing the distinction between accountability and answerability in relation to educational research, Patel asks readers to consider the concept of "ownership." Who owns knowledge, curriculum, and the purposes for learning? Such questions challenge the idea that curriculum is innocent or value-neutral, and remind us that it is constructed by and for the perpetuation of particular ways of thinking and being. Curriculum is culture; and if it is not interrogated, enacted curriculum is allowed to maintain ownership of its inherent cultural capital.

The consequences of unquestioned curriculum are substantial. Student performance on standardized assessments, for example, which are an external accountability mechanism, results in what are commonly referred to as **achievement gaps**. The achievement gap refers to disparities in academic performance that relate to student characteristics, such as race, gender, native language, and socioeconomic status, among others. In conjunction with standardized test scores, the achievement gap is demonstrated by disproportionate placements in gifted or advanced placement courses, high school and college graduation rates, and completion of graduate and professional programs. Student characteristics demarcate the achievement gap, but many factors have been shown to contribute, including "the nature of the curriculum and the school…and the pedagogical practices of teachers" (Ladson-Billings, 4). These contributing factors provide a fuller picture of the context of education, but they fall short in terms of answerability. In reality, students have unequal access to factors that affect their achievement, and describing the inequity as a "gap" focuses on expectations, but conceals responsibility and distorts reporting. Ladson-Billings calls for a more accountable description of the conditions that create the achievement gap. She argues that "We do not have an achievement gap; we have an education debt" (5). Ladson-Billings extends her argument by explaining "that the historical, economic, sociopolitical, and moral decisions and policies that characterize our society have created an education debt" (5). From a historical perspective, for example, an education debt has been incurred by laws that prevented enslaved Black people from learning to read; by mandatory residential schools where Native American children were expected to disavow family, language, and culture; by communities and schools segregated by race; and by college admissions practices that privileged White, upper-class applicants. Each of the categories of debt is buttressed by an abundance of evidence, data that support achievement deficits as consequences of social policies and practices. Further, reframing achievement gaps as educational debts points toward answerability, rather than accountability. The education system is answerable to learners, and especially to learners whose communities have experienced inequities related to discriminatory social policies. Greater accountability, through reform policies that focus on outcomes rather than inputs, will continue to exacerbate achievement gaps without addressing the educational debts that are the root cause. Educational institutions in a pluralistic society must strive to be accountable to the public and answerable to communities and learners.

Curriculum in English Classrooms

Like all disciplines, English language arts represents particular sets of knowledge and skills. NCTE couples literacy with education in its statement about the role of English teachers in challenging injustice: "As literacy educators we work every day to advance access, power, agency, affiliation, and impact for all learners." (Travel Advisory). The field of English education involves conceptual knowledge such as rhetoric; applied knowledge, such as grammar and syntax; and skills, such as reading comprehension and public speaking. Content in English classrooms tends to involve texts, including fiction and nonfiction prose, poetry, and digital products – all of which can be generated by students or used as the basis of constructing meaning. In general, the skills associated with English classrooms are reading, writing, speaking, and listening.

These skills, the fundamentals of literacy practices, begin to develop at birth and continue to grow and change over the course of a lifetime. Most children begin to learn to read by first learning to understand and produce language, and then becoming aware that symbols can be associated with language and meaning. Children can interpret and produce spoken and written language when they are very young, but literacy development does not end there. Throughout child-hood, adolescence, and adulthood, people continue to extend literacy skills. These skills, which are fostered in English classrooms, transcend school walls; people develop facility with discourses related to family, community, and work-place cultures. They create meanings from symbols in formal and informal settings that may not relate to academic literacy practices. Such literacy practices are valuable in their own right, and they also serve as a foundation for the development of academic literacy. Linguistic diversity, like all forms of diversity, is a strength, not a deficit. As Nieto reminds us, "no language is a deficit language but instead that language in whatever form is a valuable and valid means of communication that must be cherished." Language can be a weapon of oppression or a tool for liberation. It is therefore essential for English teachers to 1) appreciate English language arts as a **spiral curriculum** in which knowledge and skills are con-tinuously grown; 2) explicitly cultivate the tools necessary for students to become adept at shifting literacy practices related to different discourses; and 3) value literacy proficiencies that learners bring to school.

Built on the recognition that sophisticated, interwoven abilities are learned through recurrent practice, a spiral curriculum revisits knowledge and skills in different and increasingly complex contexts. For example, students can be intro-duced to the conventions of writing by transcribing one another's speech and then adding punctuation. Young children may focus on use of periods, question marks, and exclamation points, while older students could be expected to also use semicolons, colons, ellipses, and commas. The learning target for these lessons is similar, but the expectations are different. The same is true for reading, which is a skill that continues to develop as readers are exposed to various texts in formal and informal settings. Skill in speaking and writing, likewise, can evolve well into adulthood as people face more challenging applications of these practices.

The potential scope of an English curriculum is evident, and can be demon-strated through a simple exercise. As noted earlier, if one hundred English teachers were asked to identify ten books that every high school student should read, the result would likely be a lengthy list – as many as 1,000 texts. Teachers' educational and cultural experiences shape their decisions. The extent to which teachers can make curricular decisions varies depending on district, school, and department policies. But understanding that *all* curricula are social constructions, outcomes of decisions made by stakeholders with diverse purposes, can empower teachers. Written curricula are transformed into delivered curricula, which are then experienced by learners as received curricula. All these phases create space for originality, inspiration, and imagination. Learners can learn about drama by reading a play, watching a performance, performing a published play, and performing a play they have written. They can interpret a poem, identify literary elements, and integrate symbols into creative writing. Knowledge and skills can be cultivated through pedagogical approaches that are accountable to society and answerable to learners. This philosophy is consistent with NCTE's vision statement, which states "NCTE and its members will apply the power of language and literacy to actively pursue justice and equity for all students and the educators who serve them."

Assessing Learning

Teaching English is deliciously limitless. New texts are written every day, and language is almost endlessly malleable. Language reflects society and can be a mechanism for change. These characteristics, as seductive as they are for teachers, complicate how English is taught and especially how it is assessed. As shown in the anecdote about teaching the dog to whistle, assessment is an opportunity for students to demonstrate learning. Without assessment, teaching effectiveness remains mysterious. However, assessment is inextricable from curriculum: its complexity corresponds to the complexity of the content and skills being taught. Therefore, assessment in English language arts should be as multifaceted and authentic as the discipline. Upholding these principles are NCTE's Framing Statements on Assessment, which are based on the following beliefs:

- Assessment must include multiple measures and must be manageable.
- Consumers of assessment data should be knowledgeable about the things the test data can and cannot say about learning.
- Teachers and schools should be permitted to select site-specific assessment tools from a bank of alternatives and/or to create their own.

Regardless of intentions to adhere to these beliefs, in an era dominated by standardized assessments as mechanisms of accountability teachers may feel pressured to "teach to the test." This pressure often translates into "drill and kill" pedagogies, meaning that isolated skills are practiced and assessed in ways that are generally disconnected from authentic applications that are relevant to learners. This may play out through lessons that are sequenced without consideration of what students need to know, and want to know, and already know. Isolated vocabulary lists, taught by memorizing published definitions and assessed by matching or multiple choice tests, have been not been shown to improve students' reading comprehension or their writing lexicons. Instead of teaching definitions of lists of decontextualized words in preparation for a test, students can be taught strategies for expanding their vocabularies, and provided with opportunities for learning not just definitions, but how new words "fit into the world" (Stahl, 95). Authentic curriculum includes opportunities for authentic assessments, assessments that enable students to use literacy practices to identify and address issues that matter to them.

Since standardized assessments are often linked to credentials, teachers may feel obliged to prepare students to perform well on them, despite decades of research showing that achievement on standardized assessment corresponds to privilege. Use of standardized assessments for high-stakes decisions allows tests to serve as gatekeepers (Au; Nichols and Berliner; Dorn). Moreover, as tests are increasingly used to predict "college and career readiness," poor performance contributes to a self-fulfilling prophecy in which assessment results become intertwined with students' academic identities (Gunzenhauser). In these ways, standardized assessments contribute to the achievement gap, providing pseudo-scientific "evidence" that some learners are more capable than others.

Challenging inequities related to high-stakes standardized testing requires teachers to adopt a dual stance of **critical compliance** and **reflective resistance**. The distinction is subtle, but important, and is relevant when teachers are asked to implement policies that contradict their professional judgment. Taubman described this as having to "disavow" knowledge, and argues that such conditions damage professional identities by forcing teachers to work against the ethical and moral imperatives that called them to the field. When faced with a mandate to disavow professional principles, teachers can analyze the situation and determine which path is preferable, retaining a sense of agency and the best interests of their learners. Critical compliance involves implementing the mandate, but with a transparently critical disposition that centers on justice. For example, students can be prepared for a standardized assessment through many pedagogical approaches, some of which involve developing familiarity with the format and structure of the test. Teachers can address these skills uncritically, portraying the assessment as a natural part of schooling. Or, they can enact critical compliance, presenting the test as a structural barrier and an opportunity to use instruction to deconstruct a discriminatory mandate. A third option is reflective resistance. There are times when, after reflecting on potential consequences, resistance to policies makes sense – especially when supportive coalitions can be built. Resistance can involve subversive activities that are public or covert; however, actions are utterly ethical, painstakingly considered, and grounded in professional principles. Critical compliance and reflective resistance provide avenues for educators to act as public intellectuals, modeling a democratic process that values dissent *and* builds consent through communication.

Assessment is evidence of what students have learned, and – intended or not – reveals elements of the explicit, implicit, hidden, delivered, and received curriculum. Assessments offer a concrete glimpse of curricular consequences, since it is widely understood that what gets tested is what gets taught. This axiom reinforces the importance of ongoing analysis of how student learning is evaluated and what this evaluation reveals about practice.

Summary

Curricular decisions in English classrooms matter. Skills, knowledge, and dispositions toward language and literacy are developed, in part, through the curricular and pedagogical approaches of their teachers. As the front line in education, teachers know that a taught curriculum is fictitious if it is not connected to students' learning. In English classes, students can learn that their literacy practices matter, and they can also learn that language practices are associated with power and privilege. Content knowledge and skills are connected to social class and cultural capital, and since language is deeply connected to community and identity, how it is treated in school is consequential for students. Teachers scaffold curriculum by building relationships, providing motivation with relevant curriculum and opportunities for success, and developing capacity with meaningful, challenging content. When such scaffolding is coupled with instruction that is committed to answerability and authenticity, curriculum and assessment can begin to interrupt inequities.

Extension Questions

1. Locate a curriculum guide for secondary English and apply a critical perspective to analyze it. Consider the following questions in relation to the curriculum:

   a How were curriculum decisions made? What aspects of cultural capital are revealed in these decisions?

   b Who benefits? Whose knowledges are privileged?

   c Who loses? Whose knowledges are subjugated or omitted?

2. Revise excerpts from the curriculum analyzed in question 1 to reflect a more culturally sustaining pedagogical approach (see Chapter 2). Explain how the revisions might influence the experiences of teachers and learners.

3. Examine a secondary English lesson, using the questions below as a guide.

   a What knowledge and skills are students intended to learn?

   b How will they demonstrate this learning (how is the learning assessed)?

   c Explain how a teacher can use the results of the lesson to exhibit both *accountability* and *answerability*.

4. Reflect on your own experiences of schooling and identify how the null curriculum and the extra curriculum affected those experiences. How did these curricula reflect cultural values? How might these values have influenced the schooling of learners?

5. Review recent news articles addressing educational policies that might cause teachers to disavow professional knowledge. Discuss how teachers might use critical compliance or reflective resistance to ensure that policy decisions do not undermine efforts toward equity and justice.

Works Cited

Alim, H. Samy. *Roc the Mic Right: The Language of Hip Hop Culture*. Abingdon, UK: Routledge, 2006.

Anyon, Jean. "Social Class and the Hidden Curriculum of Work." *The Journal of Education*, vol. 162, no. 1, pp. 67–92, 1980. www.jstor.org/stable/42741976.

Apple, Michael W. "The Politics of Official Knowledge: Does a National Curriculum Make Sense?" *Teachers College Record*, vol. 95, no. 2, pp. 222–241, 1993.

Aronowitz, Stanley and Henry A. Giroux. *Education Still Under Siege*. Westport, CT: Greenwood Publishing Group, 1993.

Au, Wayne. "Social Studies, Social Justice: W(h)ither the Social Studies in High-Stakes Testing?" *Teacher Education Quarterly*, vol. 36, no. 1, 2009.

Blake, Bud. *Tiger*. 1965–2003.

Bourdieu, Pierre. "Cultural Reproduction and Social Reproduction." In *Knowledge, Education and Social Change: Papers in the Sociology of Education* (R. Brown, Editor), pp. 71–112. Tavistock, UK: Tavistock Publications, 1973.

Dorn, Sherman. *Accountability Frankenstein: Understanding and Taming the Monster*. Charlotte, NC: Information Age Publishing, 2007.

English, Fenwick W. *Deciding What to Teach and Test: Developing, Aligning, and Leading the Curriculum*. Newbury Park, CA: Corwin, 2010.

Gunzenhauser, Michael G. *The Active/Ethical Professional: A Framework for Responsible Educators*. London, UK: A&C Black, 2012.

Ladson-Billings, Gloria. "From the Achievement Gap to the Education Debt: Understanding Achievement in U.S. Schools." *Educational Researcher*, vol. 35, no. 7, pp. 3–12, October 2006. www.jstor.org/stable/3876731.

National Council of Teachers of English. *Framing Statements on Assessment*. 2004. www2.ncte.org/statement/assessmentframingst/.

National Council of Teachers of English. *NCTE Response to the NAACP Travel Advisory for the State of Missouri*. 2017. www.ncte.org/press/naacptraveladvisory.

National Council of Teachers of English. *NCTE Vision Statement*. 2017. www.ncte.org/mission/vision.

Nieto, Sonia. "Language Is Never Neutral." Heinemann, 2016. https://blog.heinemann.com/language-never-neutral/.

Nichols, Sharon L. and David C. Berliner. *Collateral Damage: How High-Stakes Testing Corrupts America's Schools*. Cambridge, MA: Harvard Education Press, 2007.

Patel, Leigh. *Decolonizing Educational Research: From Ownership to Answerability*. Abingdon, UK: Routledge, 2015.

Shen, Helen. "Worm-Like Movements Propel Octopus Ballet." *Nature*, November 2013.

Stahl, Steven A. "Four Problems with Teaching Word Meanings (and What to Do to Make Vocabulary an Integral Part of Instruction)." In *Teaching and Learning Vocabulary: Bringing Research to Practice* (Elfrieda H. Hiebert and Michael L. Kamil, Editors.) Mahwah, NJ: Erlbaum, pp. 72–110, 2005.

Taubman, Peter. "Educational Revolution." *Bank Street Occasional Paper Series*, no. 27, 2012.

4

HOW CAN WE TEACH TEXTS IN CONTEXT?

Michael, in his third year of teaching, is looking forward to his first opportunity to teach a 12th grade English class – the last required course before high school graduation. The curriculum has a poetry unit, which focuses on skills such as scansion and identification of literary terms. Content knowledge includes situating poets in relation to literary eras as well as understanding the first section of Dante's Divine Comedy, Inferno. *Having taught these students in grade 10, Michael knows them well, and is convinced that their reading level will be a barrier to accessing the translation of* Inferno *printed in the anthology. In addition to the content and skills addressed in the curriculum, Michael is committed to cultivating a positive disposition toward poetry, and he worries that* Inferno's *reading level may diminish student engagement in its potentially captivating content.*

To address this concern, Michael has decided to reduce the amount of reading, and couple the printed text with an interactive version of Inferno *he found online. The digital representation of the poem allows students to click on various "levels of hell" that are central to the narrative. Each click reveals images depicting characters and themes, and excerpts from the poem with explanations and interpretations of historical allusions. Instead of having students read the entire poem, Michael plans to assign groups of students to focus on particular sections of the poem, and then present their sections to the class. He also plans to supplement presentations with both the text and the digital versions. As Michael discusses this plan with colleagues, they offer support and raise concerns, which he has distilled into a set of questions:*

- *Does the reduction of the reading reflect lower expectations that reinforce tracks/ability groups?*
- *How might the dependence on technology affect the feasibility of the unit plan? Are there alternatives to the digital version, in case devices or internet access are unavailable?*
- *The Divine Comedy is a piece of literature from the 14th century. Is the digital version just an attempt to make an irrelevant part of the canon more appealing to today's youth? Would it be preferable to re-evaluate the suitability of this poem?*
- *Will providing digital access to explanations of the text diminish students' need to analyze the poem, withdrawing an opportunity to develop these skills? Or will the explanations serve to scaffold students in their own analysis?*

- *How will learning be demonstrated and assessed? This is especially relevant given the heterogeneous academic composition of the class, which includes students who receive special education services and students who were in Advanced Placement 11th grade English classes.*

As Michael considers these questions, he aims to balance the importance of knowledge, skills and dispositions, knowing that some of these students will attend prestigious universities, while others may never again enter an English classroom. How can he ensure that all their needs are met, and that their imaginations are engaged?

Drawing on the idea that "reading and writing are not a thing among them-selves… but are bound up in and with the social, cultural, political, and economic practices and ideologies of which they are a part" (Bloome, Power, Christian, Otto, Shuart-Faris, xx), this chapter examines how texts shape and are shaped by the contexts in which they are **produced, consumed**, and **re-produced**. To begin, the terms literacy and literature will be discussed, focusing on how these concepts relate to making meaning with texts. These two terms are often set in opposition to one another, and this chapter will compare and contrast the con-cepts as they are situated in social expectations. Language, literacy, and literature are representations of discourse, and as such they are continuously contested. Similarly contested are what it means to teach reading and what texts should be read.

On the surface, texts can seem to be neutral, even innocent. But this concep-tion is deceptive. Texts can be perceived as freestanding representatives of meaning, or they can be perceived as blank canvases on which meanings can be projected. And of course, identical texts can be understood and used, sometimes simultaneously, in both ways. Texts are artifacts that represent the cultures in which they are produced (think of *The Great Gatsby* as an illustration of its milieu), and they are also a mechanism for social change (*Between the World and Me*, for example, has produced possibilities for shifts in how race is understood and experienced). Because of this duality, texts can be tools for creating a "third space" in which meanings shape culture and are at the same time shaped by the cultures in which they exist. What becomes evident upon even superficial con-sideration of these ideas is that texts are complex and multilayered. As visual representations of discourse, texts represent existing culture and present possibi-lities for change. How texts are *perceived, selected* for classroom use, and *treated* in educational settings matters. In this chapter, the meanings of **texts, literacy**, and **literature** will be explored from historical and political perspectives. These dis-cussions lead to considerations of constructions of **literary canons**, which shape the work of English teachers, and **literary theories**, which shape pedagogical approaches to texts. This chapter will consider two key questions: *Who decides what counts as literature?* and *How do these decisions influence literacy practices in classrooms and in society, as a whole?* and will conclude with a set of questions designed to guide readers to deepen understandings of what canons of literature are and how they might be reimagined by English teachers.

What is Text?

Simply defined, **texts** are concrete representations of meanings. This definition, which may stretch the bounds of how English teachers envision their work, includes as "texts" written and spoken words, multimedia products, artwork of all kinds, and even units of experience. As an example of a unit of experience as text, Lovell, Duckor, and Homberg apply Joseph Harris's principles of revision to explore improvement of teaching practices. They accomplish this by treating lessons as texts and texts as lessons. That is, the act of teaching, as well as the documents that support that act, become texts to be analyzed and revised. If experiences can be texts, then virtual reality – or the digital world – can be a text too. Note that the term "text" has recently evolved into use as a noun (representing what we might read or write on electronic devices), as well as a verb (the act of creating what we read on these devices). **Digital discourse**, emerging through both text messages and various forms of social media, has its own sets of norms that shape interactions and influence learning. Message length (including its duration) and tone, as well as punctuation and images (including emojis and edited photographs) constitute an emerging and increasingly influential discourse, and that discourse permeates classroom walls. By the time you read this, digital discourses will have further evolved, and while young people deserve to be thoughtful producers and consumers of language, that is not enough. They also need to understand how and why language changes, and English classrooms are an ideal space for such understandings to be developed.

What Does It Mean To Be Literate?

A broad understanding of texts widens the field of English education. It also extends how we think about what it means to be literate. **Literacy**, again from a comprehensive perspective, is meaning-making. To be literate is to read, or make meaning from, through, and with, the texts that constitute our surroundings. People read the world around them, interpreting symbols, performances, gestures, expressions, silences, and words. An expansive conception of literacy enables teachers to frame learners as already literate – already skilled in language practices that can be further developed and extended in school. Moreover, defining literacy as meaning-making emphasizes the importance of its relevance and inherent interactivity. Finally, this definition of literacy foregrounds the contested nature of literacy, which Bishop describes as a "political battleground" (51).

One of the enduring arguments in the field involves whether English teachers are teachers of **literature** or teachers of literacy. From a critical perspective, this conflict can be made concrete by thinking about how we might frame our answers to a series of questions:

- Are we teachers of the content, milieus, and elements of texts, or teachers of the skills needed to make meanings from/with/through texts?

- Is our objective to develop and affirm learners' knowledge about authors, literary eras, and components of particular books?
- Do we intend to give student tools to become literary critics?
- Are there particular sets of tools that consumers and producers of texts need to master?

These question can be further broken down, of course, by contemplating which texts are engaged, how meanings can be demonstrated (which relates to instruction and assessment), and who makes these decisions. Engaging a **spiral curriculum** that integrates content and skills in cycles of ever-deepening evolution, English teachers ultimately seek to cultivate literacy through literature. Therefore, teaching English inhabits a space of praxis that intersects literacy and literature, and contributes to definitions of both. Sheila Black makes a cogent case for this perspective:

> To be literate in literature is to have some access to the wisdom of the past and also some sense of one's surroundings – the world both here and elsewhere, the larger context of culture, society, the ideas and ideals we live by and how and why they are formed and might change.
>
> To engage with stories and storytelling is to enter a discourse that involves questions of agency and power, questions of self and other, questions that often have no easy answers or many answers. In other words, literature is an essential handmaiden of literacy.
>
> When we speak of being a literate, educated population we are talking about more than the simple capacity to read and write; we are talking about the facility to weigh, judge, criticize, praise, deplore, celebrate, expose, examine, reflect upon and capture all the things of this world – and the ways in which literature engages us with the stuff of the world, all the reasons stories are so essential to us.
>
> And yet how can anyone be said to truly read or write without engaging first and foremost with the practice of literature – that is to say with the practice of storytelling?

Black clearly describes the interconnected nature of literacy and literature. Humans use the narrative of story to make sense of the world, and literature is an authoritative representation of a society's collective vision of its story. While the connections between literature and literacy are strong and intuitive, to examine the assumptions inherent in the field it may be helpful to think polemically about this enduring argument: Do English teachers teach reading, or do they teach texts? What do decisions about *what we teach* and *how we teach it* mean for students?

The answers to these questions inform both the roles of English teachers and definitions of literacy. That is, to what extent are people literate if they can:

- Sound out written words and say them aloud without full comprehension?
- Verbalize a coherent argument on a complex topic without being able to write it in essay form?
- Analyze characters in a dramatic performance or film without being able to read the script?
- Interpret multilayered references in a text without naming relevant literary theories?
- Create symbolic or artistic representations of a text without being able to identify literary devices?

The connections among these skills, and the **dispositions** that support their development, are evident. Being able to comprehend is essential to reading, and writing an argument can strengthen the thinking process, thus strengthening the ability to make a claim. Yet each of these questions reveals the complexities related to how meanings are made and demonstrated. Literacy is much more than reading and writing. Literacy is associated with the ability to engage with a range of texts, as well as apply knowledge related to technology, numeracy, philosophy, history, art, and science. Literacy links to cultural awareness, social interaction, and relations of power. Literacy is a set of **cultural practices** that reflect and shape our understandings of the past, our engagement with the present, and how we imagine our future.

As Paulo Freire famously stated, to be literate is to be able to "read the word and the world." Extending what this understanding of reading means, former NCTE President Ernest Morrell explains:

> So much is made of reading in our discipline of English, and it should be. Without having the ability to read, one is alienated from full access to citizenship and professional membership in our society. However, I want to make a distinction between mere decoding and reading. Of course, reading as an action subsumes all that decoding and comprehension imply; but it involves much more that is about questioning a text and its author. One of the things that I have become convinced of is that reading is something that needs to be re-taught at every level of education. Just because kids have learned basic decoding and comprehension skills in elementary school does not mean that we don't have to re-teach reading at the middle and high school levels. We can draw upon those initial skills, but reading takes on new and bold dimensions as adolescents confront texts from multiple genres and socio-historical locations. We want students to engage texts, to interrogate texts, to demand meaning from texts; to talk back to texts; to juxtapose texts with their lived experiences, with their encounters with other texts, and with their rapidly expanding ideas about people and the world. (28)

Morrell's explanation reinforces literacy as socially situated, and reading as a skill that is developed through a spiral curriculum; it is continuously revisited and grounded in the development of **critical literacy**. Critical literacy originated "as a way of understanding and critically engaging with the material economy of the present" (Bishop, 51). Through the lens of cultural studies, critical literacy has been more recently defined as "learning to read and write as part of the process of becoming conscious of one's experience as historically constructed within specific power relations" (Anderson and Irvine, 82). Critical literacy encompasses engagement with texts as representations of lived experiences. As cultural artifacts, texts constitute and reveal power relations; they can also challenge these power relations. Critical literacy practices expand learning beyond the comprehension and creation of texts, and into the realm of understanding how power is embedded into the reading and writing of texts. Because literacy is itself a set of cultural practices:

> ...simply teaching our students to be able to decode texts is not enough. Freire and Macedo (1987) offer that students, in order to be fully functioning as citizens and intellectuals, must be able to read the world and the messages it sends to them, for their own protection, and so that they may be able to contribute toward making the world the kind of place that they want it to be.
>
> *(Morell, 29)*

To make meanings from texts in academic settings requires both **receptive skills** and **expressive skills**; students must engage with a text, connect it to their own experience, interpret this connection, and then demonstrate the meanings they have constructed. This sentence is deceptively straightforward. The variables are endless: Who are the students? What are the texts; who selects them; according to what criteria? What experiences are available to learners? What interpretive tools are accessible for application? What opportunities exist for students to demonstrate knowledge and skills?

Teachers in English classrooms negotiate these variables every day, making decisions about the methods and materials they will use to help students make meanings from texts. And these decisions are not inconsequential: they are crucial. Because literacy is cultural, it signifies and carries relations of power. If we teach students to read but simultaneously teach them that reading is disconnected from their real lives, from the spaces in which their home culture is valued, we will have cultivated a learner who can read but won't. We will have developed skills but destroyed dispositions. English classrooms that fail to address the cultural components of literacy allow students to think of themselves as "illiterate" without examining the gaps in academic definitions of reading and writing. Critical literacies situate language learning within discourses of power and authority, allowing teachers and learners to ask questions and make decisions. It is therefore essential to develop literacy skills in conjunction with **critical dispositions** that empower learners as readers, writers, speakers, listeners, and thinkers. Critical dispositions involve continuous rethinking of evidence and expertise. Without critical dispositions, literacy skills are of little value; if young people learn to read, and also learn to hate reading, then schools have failed them. If students learn to write, but don't understand writing as an act of discovery and self-expression, schools have failed them. *How* students learn is as important as *what* they learn. In English classrooms, students can learn that their words are tentative representations of authority and are subject to continuous correction, or they can learn to use words in ways that shape the world.

Historical Perspective of Literacy

As mentioned, literacy can be defined narrowly, as applying technical skills related to academic reading and writing, or broadly, as thinking and reasoning across disciplines. Like curriculum, literacy is deeply connected to cultural practices and power relations in society. Literacy has been associated with citizenship and voting rights, and has been used as a means of reinforcing colonization and enslavement of people. Literacy practices are also coupled with social status. History reminds us that in many contexts only authorized people could interpret holy texts, and land has been stolen through laws written in languages that were unfamiliar to indigenous peoples. The material effects of literacy practices are significant and lasting.

Literacy practices also evolve. In the 400s BC, Athenian philosopher/teacher Socrates narrated serious concerns about the potential negative effects of written language. A believer in dialogue as a means of constructing knowledge, Socrates claimed that written words were analogous to pictures; they could evoke a superficial meaning, but were secondary to the experience of engaging with an author in much the same way as looking at an image is secondary to being *in* the scene – to participating *as part of* the scene. Socrates' apprehensions about writing are evident in the excerpt:

> [Writing] will create forgetfulness in the learners' souls, because they will not use their memories; they will trust to the external written characters and not remember of themselves. The specific which you have discovered is an aid not to memory, but to reminiscence, and you give your disciples not truth, but only the semblance of truth; they will be hearers of many things and will have learned nothing; they will appear to be omniscient and will generally know nothing; they will be tiresome company, having the show of wisdom without the reality.

In essence, Socrates predicted that written language would hinder memory, inhibit social interaction, and impede learning. Hundreds of years later in the 15th century, the availability of the printing press raised similar concerns, particularly with respect to holy texts, which were traditionally read and interpreted only by highly educated and trained clergy. Mass printing was perceived as likely to diminish the sanctity of these texts, "but the availability of Bibles in the vernacular allowed laypeople to take control of their spiritual lives and, if historians are correct, encouraged entrepreneurship in commerce and innovation in science." These examples illustrate how literacy practices are embedded in relations of power, and how literacy practices can influence relations of power and experiences of schooling.

Ancient fears about technology and literacy resonate today. With a wealth of data at our fingertips, the need to memorize content may seem obsolete, a possibility that evokes concerns among some educators. Similarly, some worry that easy access to unfiltered information may facilitate the spread of misinformation, such as the "fake news" that can infiltrate social and mass media. Ancient philosophers and contemporary educators are correct in noting that technologies influence teaching and learning. For English teachers in particular, the use of software to identify and correct writing raises questions about how – and whether – to teach spelling and grammar. The wavy red line that appears in some word processing programs can shape diction and style in ways that may remain unexamined. Thus, the kinds of literacy practices taught and learned in school must evolve with available technologies. Critical literacy, by questioning the origins and impacts of technologies, is an important means of interrogating the effects of technologies on learning.

Practices of literacy continue to evolve. While the rate of change may seem accelerated, and concerns intensified, responses to this evolution tend to remain relatively consistent. Gardner notes that changes in literacy practices tend to be interpreted as heralding either utopian or dystopian futures. Doomsayers claim that technologies will destroy reading and writing, and optimists predict new literacies as instruments that will unite people in a world of peace and justice. Gardner rejects this duality, and encourages educators to take into consideration the needs and desires of learners, the ever-changing media landscape, and the transformative nature of media. All of these are embedded in culture, and a critical theoretical perspective reminds us that increased access to literacy can result in changes in power relations.

NCTE's definition of 21st Century Literacies emphasizes the connections among society, technologies, and literacy practices.

> Literacy has always been a collection of cultural and communicative practices shared among members of particular groups. As society and technology change, so does literacy. Because technology has increased the intensity and complexity of literate environments, the 21st century demands that a literate person possess a wide range of abilities and competencies, many literacies. These literacies are multiple, dynamic, and malleable. As in the past, they are inextricably linked with particular histories, life possibilities, and social trajectories of individuals and groups.

This definition emphasizes the complexity of literacy practices, but it fails to address the ways in which English classrooms participate in the perpetuation of power relations. The related standards urge teachers to foster "Active, successful participants in this 21st century global society" who can "Develop proficiency and fluency with the tools of technology" and "Attend to the ethical responsibilities required by these complex environments." However, voices, desires, and concerns of students are absent from this statement, and opportunity standards are not considered. Not all students have access to "tools of technology," "multimedia texts," or "multiple streams of simultaneous information," all of which are listed as part of what students must have to be successful participants in global society. NCTE's definition of literacy highlights practices that are "multiple, dynamic, and malleable," but it is constructed on a foundation that omits the funds of knowledge students bring into classrooms. Students bring to schools literacy practices that are effective and meaningful for them in their communities, but may not align with the expectations of academic settings. This leads to considerations of how literacy and literature intersect.

Literacy and Literature

The simplest conception of literature is that it is an **artifact** of literacy – a representation (sometimes written, sometimes oral) of what counts as authentic and meaningful text. Much like the concept of literacy itself, definitions of literature are developed and enacted by **communities of practice**, communities whose cultural capital may differ and therefore be associated with different social status. Literacy practices cannot be separated from the definitions of literature, because ways of making meaning with particular texts are intertwined with the texts themselves. How meanings are made and demonstrated, and with what texts, connects to English classrooms, which reflect and have the potential to affect how academic canons of literature are described.

What it means to be an educated person is often characterized in terms of literacy. It would be surprising, for example, if a high school graduate in the United States had never heard of William Shakespeare or *Great Expectations*. However, if we were to ask one hundred English teachers to identify ten books that every high school graduate should read, the lists would be far from identical. What is the **literary canon**? What texts are worth reading and studying? Who makes these decisions, and on what basis?

In *The Ulysses Delusion: Rethinking Standards of Literary Merit*, Cecilia Konchar Farr traces the creation of the literary canon. Echoing the evolution of literacy, which is tied to issues of identity and power, the establishment of a literary canon by critics in the emergent United States was a mechanism of discrimination. Indeed, the printing press fueled the nascent genre of the novel. As Farr explains:

> ...the rise of the popular novel paralleled historically the rise of democracy and universal literacy in the United States (and Europe), and it benefitted

from the mass production of the industrial revolution and the influx of immigrants eager to learn English. (15)

The accessibility of popular novels served as an equalizer, as well as a means of building community. However, they did not contribute to the development of an elite **aesthetic**. In fact, the appeal, and resultant success, worked against attempts of "eighteenth and nineteenth century literary critics in the newly united states (who) were drawn to European aesthetic standards" (Farr, 16) and yearned for a similarly elite American literature. The desire to create a "serious American literary tradition" required a division between it and the democratic novels that were popular among working classes and women. American authors deemed worthy of recognition, such as Henry David Thoreau, Herman Melville, and Nathaniel Hawthorne, were perceived as having artistic merit based on "their complex language and symbol systems, careful literary allusions, stoic restraint, and serious philosophical and theological explorations" (17). Despite their critical acclaim, however, these books were not widely read. In fact, popularity among the masses worked against literary distinction. Farr explains:

> This division between what the literary and educational establishment called excellent and what most people really appreciated was certainly class based, but in the US tradition it was also deeply gendered. In some cases, the judgment was as simple as this: if women write it or read it, it probably isn't good; in other words, it's not sufficiently masculine to be American. Or this counterintuitive swipe at democracy: if too many people like it, it must be bad, too simplistic, too sensational, or (ironically) too moralistic. Usually these two overlapped because... from the beginning the most-read novels were mostly read by women. (17)

Built on standards intended to privilege elitist perspectives, on the shifting definitions of "artistic value," it is unsurprising that the canon of literature continues to be interrogated in academia, as teachers seek to cultivate a love of reading alongside "literary" texts that too often fail to appeal to learners. These conflicts remain prevalent. Consider whether the novels of Stephen King or Jodi Picoult, both extremely popular, would be included on a list of books an educated person should read. In a democracy, public schools must negotiate the challenge of preparing students to succeed in an academic system while simultaneously interrupting its elitist foundation. Haertling Thein and Beach discuss the contested nature of the canon in English classes:

> The phrase literary canon often evokes notions of one static, monolithic list of the best literature, with works agreed on by everyone who's anyone. This notion of a fixed canon is typically associated with courses offered in high school and college, and it often calls to mind "classic" literary texts such as Romeo and Juliet, Julius Caesar, The Adventures of Huckleberry Finn, The

Scarlet Letter, The Great Gatsby, To Kill a Mockingbird, and Hamlet (Applebee, 1996). Although this "classic" literary canon certainly does exist, it is not the only canon of literature teachers will encounter, nor does it (or any other canon) endure simply because those books are somehow the best or most valuable. Instead, this canon, like all others, has been and continues to be constructed by certain interest groups or critics who judge texts based on their own agendas or critical perspectives. (10)

Haertling Thein and Beach further describe various forces that influence the preservation of the classic literary canon. These include the **College Board**, and curricula such as **International Baccalaureate, Great Books**, and the **Common Core Standards**, among others. The College Board develops and administers Advanced Placement (AP) examinations in literature and composition. Other canonizing forces that affect students across grade levels are book awards, textbook and testing companies (Haertling Thein and Beach, 11). All these mechanisms perpetuate belief in a singular canon of texts that are judged as most valuable. It is further worth noting that the general public, and especially students, are absent from the judging pool. To apply a critical approach in order to remedy these conditions, teachers can collaborate with students to investigate how canons are created. Thein and Beach encourage teachers to cultivate in students the knowledge that:

> …canons are constructed by groups, organizations, and critics with particular agendas – groups who generally make selections based on the aesthetic, literary quality of a text – rather than by adolescents who are more likely to prefer texts that engage them with characters and plot development. (11)

Considerations of what counts as literature engage students and teachers directly with the politics of literacy and literature. Since canons, by definition, denote texts that represent communal value and experiences, their discussion is intimately connected with literary analysis and criticism. As such, critical investigations of canons of literature offer a meaningful means of interrogating power in language, as well as interrupting oppression and rectifying omissions.

Literacy, as a meaning-making practice, represents cultural uses of thought and language. Institutions such as schools enact cultural expectations that may, or may not, reflect the norms of the communities they serve. Academic canons, then, may signify values that conflict with those of learners. Simply put, teachers might wonder whether, and to what extent, students can "see" themselves in the texts studied in English class. Purves notes that literature in schools involves literary texts as well as related content that includes:

> …historical and background information concerning authors, texts, and the times in which they were written or that form their subject matter;

information concerning critical terminology, critical strategies, and literary theory; information of a broad cultural nature such as that emerging from folklore and mythology which forms a necessary starting point for the reading of many literary texts; and the set of critical strategies, procedures, dispositions, and routines that the community values. (163)

Determinations about what counts as literature, like definitions of literacy, rest with communities, which decide what matters, assign characteristics of value, and establish how knowledge will be demonstrated and rewarded. Student achievement with respect to literacy and literature is based on what the academic community values, which may or may not align with what students' home communities value. As Brandau states:

> There is an obvious contrast between the large body of interdependent canonical texts called literature in schools and the widely divergent conglomeration of materials associated with the practice of literacy outside of school. More important, real-life purposes, expectations, and strategies for literacy tasks, are very different from those valued in school. (4)

This is not to imply that schools should not emphasize **academic literacy**. An essential aspect of the role of schools is to induce students into **academic disciplines**, to prepare them to continue their education, if that is the path they choose. However, it is also important that students do not feel that academic success requires rejection of their own communities of practice.

Teaching the Canon: Literary Theory and Pedagogies

From a traditional perspective, an established canon of literature is what must be studied in English classes. Knowledge of this canon, including literary criticism of its elements, is considered to be an essential aspect of determining whether one is an "educated person." Canons, as defined by communities of practice, change over time and can reflect different understandings of how texts are positioned and the role of learners. Texts, for example, might be considered to be freestanding repositories of predetermined meaning. They can also be treated as artifacts, frozen in time, representing literary genres or milieu. Canons, like the texts that populate them, are dynamic and dependent on the pedagogies that reveal them to students.

Shakespearean drama, for example, can be taught as opaque and archaic, as poetry that requires dozens of footnotes that explain unfamiliar vocabulary that is tested for content knowledge. This approach may result in some students who are knowledgeable, but are also alienated from school and from this part of the Western canon. In contrast, Shakespeare can be performed by students who animate scenes using digital video. Uses of literary canons must be interrogated, then, in terms of both content and pedagogy. The content of a canon should be examined in terms of diversity of characters, ideological representation, and historical relevance. An additional consideration involves ensuring that diverse communities of literacy practice are included as central, rather than omitted or marginalized.

Theories of literature influence teaching. Beach, Appleman, Fecho, and Simon describe a range of literary theories as **text-centered, student-centered**, and **socioculturally focused**. The theories of literature shape the goals for student learning. Connecting literature to the pedagogical approaches to teaching (about) literature, Deborah Appleman identifies six critical literary theories that can serve as "lenses through which we can see texts" (189). The two theories most widely applied in schools are **New Criticism** and **Reader Response Criticism**. Each lens offers a distinctive perspective from which to interpret texts. Familiarizing students with these lenses, and then providing them with opportunities to use them with intention, can engage students with canonical and contemporary literature with an understanding of the possibilities of reader agency. That is, knowledge of how different critical traditions, when presented as options rather than imperatives, can enable learners and teachers to consider how diverse traditions intersect with power and privilege. Awareness of diverse approaches to engaging with texts can also open spaces for innovative lenses that can emerge from historically marginalized communities, as well as from the intersections of various critical traditions.

Theories related to literary criticism influence pedagogies. For example, "**close reading**," an approach widely adopted as part of the Common Core Standards, is grounded in a New Critical perspective of texts. New Criticism, which gained popularity among literary critics in the 1940s, and became increasingly widespread in the 20th century, emphasizes the content of a text over sociological or historical contexts from which it emerged and in which it is read. Delahoy asserts that:

> New Criticism emphasizes explication, or "close reading," of "the work itself." It rejects old historicism's attention to biographical and sociological matters. Instead, the objective determination as to "how a piece works" can be found through close focus and analysis, rather than through extraneous and erudite special knowledge. It has long been the pervasive and standard approach to literature in college and high school curricula.
>
> *(https://public.wsu.edu/~delahoyd/new.crit.html)*

Pedagogies related to close reading treat texts as free-standing artifacts of meaning, and the role of readers is to decode and analyze texts, seeking comprehension. In essence, from a New Critical perspective, the role of learners is to engage in close reading in order to decode texts and unlock meanings. The English language arts Common Core anchor standard 1 requires learners to "Read closely to determine what the text says explicitly and to make logical inferences from it; cite specific textual evidence when writing or speaking to support conclusions drawn from the text" (10).

Scholars in the field argue that close reading is intended for application to complex texts that lend themselves to layers of meaning that can be uncovered through multiple readings. This interpretation leads back to the notion of a canon; to warrant close reading, texts must be considered to be worthy of significant time and attention (Shanahan). A pedagogical approach based on close reading focuses on deep comprehension and precise interpretations of texts. According to Wiggins, close reading in preparation for college-level study involves two steps: 1) observations of facts, features, and rhetorical elements; and 2) interpretations of observations that logically lead to conclusions based on textual evidence. Wright, a professor of literature at the University of Pittsburgh, divides these steps into three: understanding, noticing, and explaining.

A contrasting approach to a close reading of texts involves application of the critical literary theory called Reader Response. Rather than taking readers deeper into texts, pedagogical methods based on Reader Response reach from the text into the experiences of learners. According to Appleman:

> This type of criticism does not designate any one critical theory, but focuses on the activity of reading a work of literature. Reader-response critics turn from the traditional conception of a work as an achieved structure of meanings to the responses of readers as their eyes follow a text. By this shift of perspective, a literary work is converted into an activity that goes on in a reader's mind, and what had been features of the work itself – including narrator, plot, characters, style, and structure – is less important than the connection between a reader's experience and the text. It is through this interaction that meaning is made.
>
> This is the school of thought most students seem to adhere to. Proponents believe that literature has no objective meaning or existence. People bring their own thoughts, moods, and experiences to whatever text they are reading and get out of it whatever they happen to, based upon their own expectations and ideas. (163–164)

Pedagogies related to a Reader Response approach center the experiences and perceptions of students. Teachers might employ strategies such as having students making connections (text-to-self, text-to-text, and text-to-world) or evaluate texts in relation to their own backgrounds. Assignments emphasize student reactions to the text, and then move toward including other conceptual or historical perspectives. The Reader Response approach meanings are generated in the space between learner and text. The responses of readers to texts creates meanings. This contrasts with New Criticism, which presumes that meaning already exists in texts and that the role of readers is to discover and articulate it.

Contemporary theories of literary criticism integrate relations of power into the study of texts. **Marxist theory, feminist theory, gender and queer theory,**

critical race theory, and **critical disability studies** have in common a focus on interrogating existing bodies of knowledge and investigating how literary texts reinforce and interrupt perceptions and mechanisms of power in society. Marxist criticism employs a lens that involves class differences, based on the ways that socioeconomic systems shape people's life experiences. Reading a text from this perspective might involve thinking about the social class of the author, as well as the characters, and exploring how the economic system influences the dominant and competing narratives. Feminist literary criticism seeks to expose the male-dominated patriarchal structure of Western societies and to explore how systems within this structure influence lives. Although there is a diverse array of feminist theoretical traditions, they share the belief that gender equality is the key to social change. Extending this concept, gender studies and queer theory provide a lens that breaks down the binary of male-female and emphasizes the complexity of how such categories construct identities and opportunities. This approach uncovers deeply held social assumptions about what is natural and normal, with the intent of opening possibilities through examination of the politics of gender and sexuality that are perpetuated through texts. Critical race theory (CRT) exposes and confronts how race and racism, as well as class, gender, sexual orientation, national origin, and other characteristics contribute to the narratives that construct the experiences of individuals and groups in society. CRT involves examination of a wide range of texts and artifacts that reveal the historical and contemporary effects of racism in society, as well as an orientation toward actions that effect change. Critical disability studies, as a field, looks at disability as an aspect of identity that is analogous to race, gender, and ethnicity, among others. Disability studies is a form of literary criticism that is focused on how what is viewed as "normal" is influenced by public artifacts and texts. Literary lenses such as these explicitly aspire to reveal and interrupt how relations of power and privilege end oppression and create conditions where equity and justice prevail. Integral to these approaches to literary criticism are questions that echo those related to critical theory: *What counts as knowledge? What counts as normal? Who decides? Who benefits? Who loses?*

In English classes, literary theories can offer a way of engaging with texts that integrates critical literacy with literary traditions. When made explicit, and approached in ways that value student experiences and responses while honoring the origins and intents of texts, literary theories can serve as lenses that magnify characteristics of society, as well as narratives that can interrupt inequities.

Summary

Beginning with a scenario in which a teacher faces a dilemma about how to engage students with different versions of a classical text, this chapter discussed how texts shape, and are shaped by, the contexts in which they are produced, consumed, and reproduced. This discussion involved consideration of how literacy is defined and used in communities of practice, as well as how canons of literature help to characterize what it means to be an educated person. Critical literacies were introduced as tools for interrogating the relations of power that are integrated in the creation and use of texts. Additionally, literary theories were presented as lenses for investigating how narratives contribute to the construction of society, and to the construction of identities of those in society.

This chapter provided a framework for considering how texts are consumed by readers through various lenses related to various contexts. The next chapter will explore how the production of writing influences, and is influenced by, factors involving society and identity.

Extension Questions

1. On page 52, the following claim is made:

   Texts can be perceived as freestanding representatives of meaning, or they can be perceived as blank canvases on which meanings can be projected. And of course, identical texts can be understood and used, sometimes simultaneously, in both ways.

   Think about how a text can be a "freestanding representation of meaning." What might that look like in a classroom? What teacher and student experiences would be consistent with that approach?

   Now imagine that same text as "a blank canvas on which meanings can be projected." What might that look like in a classroom? What teacher and student experiences would be consistent with that approach?

2. Reflect on key texts that influenced your secondary education. List 5–10 texts that every high school student should read. Compare your list with the similar selections generated by professional organizations, by educators, and by students. What texts recur? What texts are missing?

3. Revisit the scenario that introduces this chapter and consider the factors that Michael should consider in deciding how to plan for his classes. How do conceptions of literature and literacy relate to the curricular decisions Michael needs to make?

4. Consider the use of the term "critical" with respect to the following concepts. How are the definitions and applications of the term "critical" similar in the following contexts, and how do the terms differ?

   a Critical theory
   b Critical literacy
   c Critical literary theory

5. The relationship between theories of literature and goals for student learning is well-established (see *Teaching Literature to Adolescents* by Beach, Appleman, Fecho, Simon, 2010, especially Figure 3.1). For example, a text-centered theory of literature sees literature as the source of meaning, while a socio-cultural theory sees literature as open to various critical perspectives in relation to social contexts. Think about how these theories influence learning goals. Create student learning goals that are associated with different theories of literature, and discuss how the theories influence learning and language practices.

Works Cited

Anderson, Gary L. and Irvine, Patricia. "Informing Critical Literacy with Ethnography." In *Critical Literacy: Politics, Praxis, and the Postmodern* (Colin Lankshear and Peter L. McLaren, Editors). Albany, NY: SUNY Press, pp. 81–104, 1993.

Apartment 46. *Socrates Was Against Writing.* May 2011. http://apt46.net/2011/05/18/socra tes-was-against-writing/

Appleman, Deborah. *Critical Encounters in High School English: Teaching Literary Theory to Adolescents.* New York, NY: Teachers College Press, 2000.

Beach, Richard, Deborah Appleman, Bob Fecho, and Rob Simon. *Teaching Literature to Adolescents.* Abingdon, UK: Routledge, 2010.

Bishop, Elizabeth. "Critical Literacy: Bringing Theory to Praxis." *Journal of Curriculum Theorizing*, vol 30, no. 1, pp. 51–63, 2014.

Black, Sheila. "Gemini Ink: Connecting Literacy and Literature." *The Rivard Report*, March 2013. https://therivardreport.com/gemini-ink-connecting-literacy-and-literature/

Bloome, David, Stephanie Power Carter, Beth Morton Christian, Sheila Otto, and Nora Shuart-Faris. *Discourse Analysis and the Study of Classroom Language and Literacy Events: A Microethnographic Perspective.* Abingdon, UK: Routledge, 2004.

Brandau, Deborah. *Literacy and Literature in School and Non-School Settings.* Albany, NY: National Research Center on English Learning & Achievement, 1996.

Common Core State Standards Initiative. *Conventions of Standard English*, 2017. www.cor estandards.org/ELA-Literacy/

Delahoyde, Michael. *New Criticism.* https://public.wsu.edu/~delahoyd/new.crit.html.

Farr, Cecilia Koncharr. *The Ulysses Delusion: Rethinking Standards of Literary Merit.* Basingstoke, UK: Palgrave Macmillan, 2016.

Gardner, Howard. "The End of Literacy? Don't Stop Reading." *The Washington Post*, February 2008.

Haertling Thein, Amanda and Richard Beach. "*Critiquing and Constructing Canons in Middle Grade English Language Arts Classrooms.*" *Voices from the Middle*, vol. 21, no. 1, September 2013.

Lovell, Jonathan, Brent Duckor, and Carrie Holmberg. "Rewriting Our Teaching Practices in Our Own Voices." *English Journal*, vol. 104, no. 6, pp. 55–60, July 2015.

National Council of Teachers of English. *The NCTE Definition of 21st Century Literacies.* February 2013. www2.ncte.org/statement/21stcentdefinition/.

Morrell, Ernest. "English Teaching as Teaching Students to Read the Word and the World." *The Council Chronicle*, November 2014.

Purves, Alan. *The Idea of Difficulty in Literature Learning*. Albany, NY: State University of New York Press, 1991.

Shanahan, Timothy. "What is Close Reading?" *Shanahan on Literacy*, June 2012. http://sha nahanonliteracy.com/blog/what-is-close-reading#sthash.Iukm6HuS.dpbs.

Wright, Jarrell D. "How to Teach Close Reading: Demystifying Literary Analysis for Undergraduates." *Teaching College Literature*. http://teachingcollegelit.com/tcl/?page_ id=255.

5

BEING AND BECOMING WRITERS

Who Can Be an Author?

"Writing is just one of those things that can't be taught," Cherie, the chair of the high school English department said. "You can tell right away which students are going to be really good writers, and which ones are going to have to struggle to achieve basic competency." Jewell paused, repeating the words to herself silently to ensure she had heard correctly. Was it possible that her colleague and department leader honestly believed that writing could not be taught?

Cherie, reading doubt in Jewell's expression, continued. "Of course, we can teach students to memorize spelling words, to use punctuation correctly, and to include topic sentences in their paragraphs, but as far as being a real writer, you can tell right away who has it and who doesn't. Some students just have a talent for language, just like some have a talent for sports or music."

"Those are interesting comparisons," Jewell nodded, "and of course talent is relevant to achievement. But athletes in all sports benefit from instruction and coaching. Music teachers teach lessons at practically every level. And both sports and music provide lots of opportunities for meaningful performance, alongside instruction and practice. We have to let students discover how they can learn from writing, and let them write in ways that are meaningful to them. They need real audiences and purposes for writing, and then they will care about conventions."

"You know," Cherie replied, "we are not really disagreeing. Once students have the basics, once they can write a correct sentence, and then put sentences together into paragraphs, then they can start to experiment and find their own voices. Athletes learn drills, and musicians learn scales, right? If student don't learn how to write right, no one will care what they are trying to say."

Jewell spoke hesitantly. "But students already know how to communicate, and they already have thoughts. If we spend too much time correcting their writing, they'll just learn to hate it. And maybe they will never find their voices. I think that writing can be taught, but that it has to start with honoring the literacy practices they bring to our classrooms."

Cherie shook her head firmly. "Your ideas are good, but they are in the wrong order. Students need to know the rules first, and then they can learn how to express themselves within the rules. And as I said, real writers are just born that way."

"Actually," Jewell spoke softly but with conviction, "real writers are not born. They are taught."

As is discussed throughout this book, power, discourse, and identity are inextricably interrelated. Language, as a component of discourse, influences how we perceive the world and how we interact within it. Gee argues that "any technology, including writing, is a cultural form, a social product whose shape and influence depend on prior political and ideological factors" (58). This chapter will investigate how different conceptions of writing affect experiences and practices of writing. It will explore different conceptions of what it means to author, writing as a **product** and a **process**, the roles of emotion and cognition in composition, and the interconnections of skills and content in writing instruction.

Writing can be used to assess knowledge and skills, and it can be a pedagogy of discovery. It can be taught as a vehicle for developing competence in genres, or a vehicle for social transformation. Enduring arguments about writing in the English classroom include discussions of **instrumental** and **exploratory** purposes of writing, as well as the interplay of **form** and **function** in written communication. The chapter will consider how writing, thinking, and **identity construction** are mutually influential, as well as how the social purposes of writing, inside and outside the classroom, affect how students and teachers perceive and use processes of writing.

Writing and Thinking

While it is clear that the ways people think affect their use of language, it is a more subtle notion that the ways people use language affect their thinking. As an artifact of discourse, reading can shape thinking by contributing to ideas, by expanding the **schema**, or patterns of thoughts and knowledge, that we already possess. The deeper and more diverse reading experiences are, the richer our schema becomes. Reading, therefore, influences our thinking. Writing, however, can be perceived as either a static artifact of thought or a process that both reveals and shapes thinking. This fundamental tension in how writing is conceived affects every aspect of writing, from composition to assessment, and because writing is a mechanism of literacy and discourse, how it is experienced by learners affects their academic achievement, identity formation, and social class identification.

Emphasizing the connection between writing and thinking and the importance of this idea for educators, Moffett equates writing with inner speech:

> Educators would do best ... to conceive of writing, first of all, as full-fledged authoring, by which I mean authentic expression of an individual's own ideas, original in the sense that he or she has synthesized them for him or herself.... Presupposing true authorship ... acknowledges that *any* writing [emphasis in original] about whatever personal or impersonal subject, for whatever audience and purpose, can never comprise anything but some focused and edited version of inner speech. The chief reason for defining writing as a revision of inner speech is to ensure that writing be

acknowledged as nothing less than thinking, manifested a certain way, and to make sure that it is taught accordingly (88–89)

For writing to be learned as an act of knowledge construction and discovery that involves the expression of original ideas, it cannot be perceived as strictly a pre-determined product. Moffett continues, noting the importance of focusing on both the visible and the invisible aspects of composition:

> Generally, the materialistic bias of our culture practically forces us to prefer the visible domain of language forms … to the invisible domain of thought, which is still a scary can of worms. But teachers have no business preferring either and have no choice but to work *in the gap* [emphasis in original] between thought and speech. Writing is a manifestation of thought, but, however tempting, we cannot deal with it only as it finally manifests itself visually in writing. (89)

The key challenge, then, is to support both the visible and the invisible aspects of writing. To do this requires a conception of writing as both process and product, and to see both as related to identity construction and social interaction. Since writing shapes thinking, classroom experiences and practices of writing can have a profound influence on students' conceptions of themselves as literate participants in social discourse. School experiences have a powerful influence on the development of young people as writers; consequently, writing instruction impacts identity development.

Who Can Be an Author?

The tensions between writing as a means of demonstrating knowledge and writing as a tool for discovery and constructing knowledge is threaded through historic debates in the field. In broad strokes, Peter Elbow and David Bartholomae represent positions that may be helpful in tracing the frame of the debate about teaching writing. Their dispute, which began in the 1990s and focused on undergraduate composition, centers on the role of teachers in writing instruction, how writers are positioned as they develop, and what processes best support academic achievement in writing. Bartholomae's claim is that teachers are essential to the development of writers. The role of teachers is to provide training in the discourse of academic writing. From this standpoint, writers gain power by situating their products in the historical and cultural context of existing work. Writers must demonstrate competency and expertise before they can be taken seriously; in a sense, aspiring writers must be inducted and demonstrate their skills prior to becoming writers. Bartholomae emphasizes the social nature of writing, highlighting the ways in which all writing involves, to some extent, engagement in dialogue with other writers. He explains:

> Thinking of writing as academic writing makes us think of the page as crowded with others... that our writing is not our own, nor are the stories we tell when we tell the stories of our lives—they belong to TV, to Books, to Culture and History. To offer academic writing as something else is to keep this knowledge from our students... to keep them from confronting the particular representations of power, tradition and authority reproduced whenever one writes. (63–64)

Bartholomae underscores the importance of teachers as guides who can provide the background and skills learners need in order to earn their place as writers. He argues that teachers do students a disservice when they do not teach them the discursive norms of academic writing. He states that these students "are not so much trapped in a private language as they are shut out from one of the privileged languages of public life, a language they are aware of but cannot control" (9). The teacher's role, then, is to provide students with instruction that will enable them to write in ways that will influence a range of audiences. To do this, writers must practice and learn the conventions of academic literacy first, to establish themselves as members of the community. Such members require mastery of discourse connected to privilege.

> I think that all writers, in order to write, must imagine for themselves the privilege of being "insiders"—that is, of being both inside an established and powerful discourse, and of being granted a special right to speak. And I think that right to speak is seldom conferred upon us—upon any of us, teachers or students—by virtue of the fact that we have invented or discovered an original idea. (67)

In arguing for more intentional induction of what he terms "**basic writers**" into the community of academic writers, Bartholomae suggests two approaches. One begins with explicit instruction that demystifies academic conventions of writing. Such instruction would involve assignments that scaffold and approximate disciplinary discourse. The other approach begins with an examination of student writing that seeks to identify discrepancies between these products and selected exemplars. Instruction would focus on systematic targeting of errors to resolve common problems. Bartholomae ultimately argues for the importance of writing as a socioculturally situated tool for students to develop their voice, and he privileges critical writing over personal narrative.

Both Elbow and Bartholomae understand writing as a form of thinking related to power and privilege. Their debate is framed around a difference in focus and succession. Bartholomae asserts that writers must first master the conventions of writing, so as to be able to participate with necessary privilege. Elbow, on the other hand, claims that participants in any community of literacy practice are already writers, and that they can develop competency through exploration and presentation of their own ideas. Elbow asserts that beginning with the idea that the domain of "real" writing belongs in the academic community creates a sense of helplessless. He describes this *misconception* of writing as follows:

> Writing is a two-step process. First you figure out your meaning, then you put it into language. Most advice we get either from others or from ourselves·follows this model: first try to figure out what you want to say; don't start writing till you do; make a plan; use an outline; begin writing only afterward. Central to this model is the idea of keeping control, keeping things in hand. Don't let things wander into a mess. The commonest criticism directed at the process of writing is that you didn't clarify your thinking ahead of time; you allowed yourself to go ahead with fuzzy thinking; you allowed yourself to wander; you didn't make an outline. (14)

Elbow's conception of writing is in concert with Moffett's discussion of writing as inner speech, or thought. Elbow disrupts the notion of writing as a product by focusing on writing as a way of thinking, exploring, and discovering unexpected ideas.

> Instead of a two-step transaction of meaning-into-language, think of writing as an organic, developmental process in which you start writing at the very beginning—before you know your meaning at all—and encourage your words gradually to change and evolve. Only at the end will you know what you want to say or the words you want to say it with. You should expect yourself to end up somewhere different from where you started. Meaning is not what you start out with, with but what you end up with. (15)

In this approach to writing, teachers serve as facilitators who create opportunities for students to write, and write, and write some more. A proponent of **freewriting**, especially for beginners, Elbow claims that "It's at the beginnings of things that you most need to get yourself to write a lot and fast" (16). This reduces anxiety and allows time and space for thoughts to expand and clarify. When you write for exploration, "you must start by writing the *wrong meanings in the wrong words*; but keep writing till you get to the right meanings in the right words. Only at the end will you know what you are saying" (16). Elbow further contends that the strategy "start writing and keep writing" (30) allows for greater fluency and deeper meanings to emerge. He notes: "Producing writing, then, is not so much like filling a basin or pool once, but rather getting water to keep flowing through till finally it runs clear" (28). Elbow's approach allows (or requires) writers to become comfortable with the "chaos and disorientation" of the early phases of writing so that a "center of gravity" of meaning might emerge. While useful at the start of a writing project, freewriting supports the production of meaning at any phase of the process. That is, outlining and freewriting are not mutually exclusive activities; a writer might begin with an outline, and then freewrite within the frame of the outline.

The difference between the approaches that Bartholomae and Elbow espouse involves, in a sense, who becomes an author, and how. Is it necessary to first become fluent in academic discourse, where authorship is determined on the basis of earning this privilege? Or is it preferable to develop initial fluency in developing one's own thoughts and ideas, and then perhaps shifting the discourse of privilege to reflect greater diversity of thought and experience? These questions offer a starting point for thinking about teaching writing in English classes. From a critical theoretical perspective, they illustrate different ways to answer questions about who decides what it means to be a writer, and these decisions relate to whether writing is treated primarily as a product or a process.

Writing: Product and Process

Deliberations about teaching writing on the basis of its product or teaching writing as a process have a long history in the field. In the early 1970s, writing teacher and scholar Donald Murray emphasized the benefits of teaching writing as a process. He described writing as

> ...the process of discovery through language. It is the process of exploration of what we know and what we feel about what we know through language. It is the process of using language to learn about our world, to evaluate what we learn about our world, to communicate what we learn about our world. Instead of teaching finished writing, we should teach unfinished writing, and glory in its unfinishedness. (4)

Murray believed that teaching writing as a product underscores an error-based approach that ultimately hinders the development of writing. Here, he explains how a product-based orientation to writing instruction can emerge:

> Most of us are trained as English teachers by studying a product: writing. Our critical skills are honed by examining literature, which is finished writing; language as it has been used by authors. And then, fully trained in the autopsy, we go out and are assigned to teach our students to write, to make language live.
>
> Naturally, we try to use our training. It's an investment and so we teach writing as a product. (3)

Training in literary analysis is one reason that teaching writing as a product prevails. Another reason involves the widespread use of standardized assessment. As **standardized assessments** increasingly determine academic achievement, **product-oriented** approaches to writing instruction are escalating. This is an expected consequence of having student and teacher competency assessed on the basis of an artifact rated on a common scale. A product-centered approach to writing instruction accentuates the mechanical aspects of writing, which tend to be easier to score than content. Product-orientation is often associated with **formulaic writing**, which can be an effective way to improve scores on standardized assessments. Writing instruction based on formulas seems to enable students to address complex tasks; however, they tend to lead students to see writing as a "fill-in-the-blank" activity, thus reducing the need for thinking and the opportunity for discovery. Formulaic writing can provide sentence-level support, such as thesis statement prototypes, and paragraph-level scaffolds, such as the Shaffer method (1995), ACE (Answer/Cite evidence/Explain), and RAGE (Restate/Answer/Give example/Explain). It can also offer guidance for larger products, such as the five-paragraph essay, the "story hamburger," and templates for particular essay genres. An example of the utility of this approach can be illustrated by a prompt from a previous New York State Regents Examination in English Language Arts. Students were required to pass the examination in order to graduate; the prompt called the "Critical Lens" was one of four writing assignments on the assessment. An example of a critical lens essay prompt, which exemplifies a literary-based product approach to writing, is provided below:

> Your Task: Write a critical essay in which you discuss two works of literature you have read from the particular perspective of the statement that is provided for you in the Critical Lens. In your essay, provide a valid interpretation of the statement, agree or disagree with the statement as you have interpreted it, and support your opinion using specific references to appropriate literary elements from the two works.
> "Show me a hero and I will write you a tragedy."
> — *F. Scott Fitzgerald* The Crack-Up*, 1945 New Directions*

Critical Lens Guidelines: Be sure to

- Provide a valid interpretation of the critical lens that clearly establishes the criteria for analysis
- Indicate whether you agree or disagree with the statement as you have interpreted it
- Choose two works you have read that you believe best support your opinion
- Use the criteria suggested by the critical lens to analyze the works you have chosen
- Avoid plot summary. Instead, use specific references to appropriate literary elements (for example: theme, characterization, setting, point of view) to develop your analysis
- Organize your ideas in a unified and coherent manner

- Specify the titles and authors of the literature you choose
- Follow the conventions of standard written English

This on-demand, timed writing assignment requires students to complete a series of tasks in one product. They must interpret the quote, agree or disagree, and support their position with references to literary elements from two texts. While each part of the task is not particularly difficult, the combination of components, in a time-sensitive, high-stakes setting, led many teachers to provide scaffolded, formulaic approaches to this essay. Further complicating the conditions was the fact that teachers were forbidden to score their own students' work. As in many classrooms, formulaic writing was perceived as a way of supporting students in achieving success and in earning credentials.

Although its appeal is understandable, especially in relation to standardized assessment, Kameen identifies four significant problems with formulaic writing. It removes inquiry from the writing process, it diminishes student agency with respect to writing, and its negative effects disproportionately affect students who are already marginalized, such as English language learners and others whose literacy practices most differ from those used in school. Writing instruction that is product-oriented and formulaic puts form before function. It privileges the frame and the format over the ideas and the content, and it devalues the activity of writing as also a process of thinking. In a sense, in a product-focused, formulaic approach to writing, the map is more important than the journey.

When writing instruction is oriented to a process, form follows function. Writing begins with purposes that originate from learners, and the audience and genre are determined in reference to these purposes. Kameen, who teaches 8th grade English, elaborates on how such an approach works in his classroom, and provides an example to illustrate it:

> Outside of the use of formulas in my classroom, I ask students to begin *first* by generating ideas *before* offering them structural support to best serve those ideas. The key in this type of writing instruction is shifting the purpose of writing aggressively towards the process of inquiry and discovery, by positioning their writing within the context of real literacy practices (meaning, practices that are actually meant to be used in life outside of the classroom).
>
> For example, my classroom's primary curriculum project throughout the year asks students to:
>
> 1 Identify a real need within a community.
> 2 Design an innovative plan to meet this real need.
> 3 Implement their plan to create real change.
>
> Within the scope of this design-cycle, writing is positioned as a powerful form of expression meant to effect actual change in the world, as opposed to a performance of formulaic writing compliance. By doing so, the hope is that

my students become aware that different structures and genres of writing can be used to support their ideas in powerful ways.

From a critical theoretical perspective, it is important to interrogate how pre-determined forms might affect thinking and writing. Such interrogation leads to considerations about modes of writing.

Multimodal Writing

Like reading, writing is influenced by **New Literacy Studies**, which have expanded modes of receptive and expressive engagement with texts. Miller and McVee describe how the perspective of New Literacy Studies extends under-standings of "**composition**" to include the creation of a broad range of texts. Texts, socially constructed artifacts of expression, can include traditional linguistic modes such as essays and poetry, as well as sound, images, and even movement. As modes of communication evolve, **digital literacies** generated through a variety of devices are also shaping **multimodal composition**, creating oppor-tunities for students to make meaning with **digital video** or **3D printing**, for example. While innovative digital technologies tend to garner attention in the field, it is important to keep in mind that technologies are tools for learning, and multimodal composition can involve simple technologies such as crayons, clay, food, and fabric. Multimodal composition, at its essence, requires teachers and students to reimagine thought and expression of meaning in terms of purpose, audience, and context.

One shift that Miller and McVee make evident is the use of the term "**design**" with respect to expression of meaning. More than "composition," design evokes innovation in both form and function. Thinking about making meaning as a process of design opens space for reimagining modes of writing, emphasizing innovation and possibility over competence and conventions. In this way, the metaphor of writing as design is more inclusive of diverse voices, cultures, and literacy practices. When the shape of the product is designed by learners, writing necessarily becomes taught as a process.

Critics of this approach express concern that echoes Bartholomae's perspective of academic writing, and can be framed through these questions: Will students who demonstrate proficiency in multimodal design and expression develop competencies connected to academic literacy? Will the **metalanguage** of digital video composition transfer to the metalanguage of research papers or academic arguments? These questions return us to the debate about whether the form or product of writing should precede, and therefore shape, the development of meaning, or whether meaning should be developed first, allowing the product to take the shape of the thinking and ideas expressed. The orientation of writing instruction with respect to these questions has a profound impact on the experiences of student writers.

Assessment, Teachers, Students, and Writing

A key point about literacy is that developmental experiences and practices influence competence in and conceptions about language. That is, how people learn to write affects their ability to write, how they imagine the purposes of writing, and how they perceive themselves as writers. How people learn to use their spoken voices influences how, and whether, they speak, sing, whisper, shout, yodel, proclaim, or scream. Consequently, if people learn that the primary purpose of writing is to repeat authoritative meanings in prescribed formats, they lose the opportunity to learn how writing can be a process of discovery, or a way to explore and make meanings from their own experiences.

In many schools today, writing instruction is driven by standardized assessment. Writing is taught formulaically, and scored according to rubrics. Some examinations, such as the SAT, include essays that are machine scored. This type of writing tends to be taught with product-oriented pedagogies, with the aim of facilitating the competencies needed to score well. Teaching to standardized tests has well-documented negative effects that are particularly detrimental to historically marginalized populations. Since most public school teachers attended public schools, their experiences of writing have been shaped by standardized assessment. They may see the purposes of writing as **instrumental** – a product-centered task intended to achieve a goal or credential; and they may not have had personal experience with writing as an **exploratory** process that can extend thinking and lead to discovery. The absence of the experience of writing as a process of discovery hinders teachers' ability to provide instruction that supports meaningful writing.

Like many teachers and researchers, Donald Graves affirms the need for teachers of writing to *be* writers. When asked what one thing teachers ought to do when teaching writing, he responded:

> Write yourself. Invite children to do something you're already doing. If you're not doing it, "Hey," the kids say, "I can't wait to grow up and not have to write, like you." They know. And for the short term and the long term, you'll be doing yourself a favor by writing. All of us need it as a survival tool in a very complex world. The wonderful thing about writing is that it separates the meaningless and the trivial from what is really important. So we need it for ourselves and then we need to invite children to do what we're doing. You can't ask someone to sing a duet with you until you know the tune yourself. (38–43)

Katie Wood Ray explains why teachers need to be practitioners of the craft of writing:

> We write so that we know what to teach about how this writing work gets done. We write so that we know what writers think about as they go

through the process. We write so that our curriculum knowledge of the process of writing runs deep and true in our teaching. We write so that we can explain it all. (3)

The ubiquity of standardized assessments can be a barrier to process-oriented writing instruction. Generations of new teachers' lived experiences of academic writing are steeped in product-oriented, formulaic practices. These conditions require a critical approach to writing instruction, an approach that investigates and interrogates how our schooling influences how we teach. Schools, as social institutions, shape identities and relationships. The purposes of our work in English classrooms, then, intersect with the purposes of schools. As educators, we must ask ourselves how our schools integrate the instrumental and exploratory purposes of school. Built on relationships, classrooms can be spaces where **cognition** and **emotion** are valued.

Standardized assessments reinforce a logic of right answers, a technical approach to writing and grammar that focuses on cognition and excludes emotion and relationships. Smagorinsky, in much of his scholarship, describes how "This technical, emotionally dry value has become instituted in federal policies that view test scores as more important than how people feel about being in school." He argues that

> ...it matters to pay careful attention to how teachers and students feel about being in school. How they feel provides the foundation for how they will engage with curriculum and instruction. If school is made into an impersonal, cold, uncaring place, then it's hard to get teachers or students to care about each other or the academic disciplines that bring them together. When writing expressively is reduced to writing properly, then it's no wonder that kids feel that school is irrelevant to their lives.

An exploratory, process-oriented approach to writing need not preclude developing fluency with conventions of writing. Concerns raised about this possibility often draw on rules of grammar as examples of skills best addressed through direct instruction. Research, however, negates the effectiveness of this approach. Dunn notes that the very term "grammar" is too broad and diffusely employed to be meaningful, and that "people can mean almost anything when talking about grammar: memorizing rules or perceived rules, reciting the parts of speech, punctuating someone else's sentences, correcting spelling or usage errors on a handbook practice page, etc." According to Dunn, lack of clarity about what constitutes "grammar," and how grammar knowledge relates to writing, contributes to ineffective writing instruction. Citing decades of research, she differentiates between teaching writing coupled with teaching proofreading, and teaching grammar as a set of isolated knowledge and skills.

> Teaching editing and careful proofreading, however, is not the same as what many people think of as "teaching grammar." When well-meaning teachers

use the same old isolated grammar drills, textbook exercises, or worksheets that students' grandparents may have been subjected to when they were in school, students' writing does not improve.

Peer-reviewed research over the past fifty years has consistently shown that isolated grammar drills and worksheets do not help students improve their writing – and in some cases can make writing worse.

Teaching writing is integral to cultivating dispositions about language. As a component of discourse, it intersects with culture and influences identity construction. Thus writing, and writing instruction, relates to thinking. If students learn that writing and thinking are disconnected from their own ideas and their own communities of literacy practice, they may become alienated from their intellectual capacity. Dunn argues that instruction about the conventions of writing cannot be separated from writing as an act of making meaning. Echoing the questions that frame this chapter, she claims that:

> Good grammar instruction can occur only after the following question is taken seriously: "What is good writing instruction?" The best grammar instruction happens when students are so engaged in a writing project that they want to make it better.

When students care about their writing, when the purposes are authentic and their audiences matter, then proofreading and effective uses of conventions matter too. Without emotional, intellectual, or social engagement, writing becomes an academic exercise. Its rules seem arbitrary and pointless.

To hone their ability to be effective communicators, students need opportunities to practice and master norms associated with a range of writing communities. They need to write for different purposes and audiences, using a variety of genres and modalities, and they need to get instructive feedback on their writing in order to improve their skills. A critical approach to writing instruction requires teachers to consider this work in light of the debate between process and product. Are student writers given assignments in which they demonstrate understanding of existing knowledge, or are they provided with opportunities to discover meaning and construct knowledge? Do writing assignments hinge on repetition of authoritative information and predetermined modalities, or do they originate with authentic engagement in real-world events? Responses to these queries can offer indications about how writing is approached, and whether it is taught and learned as a means of reproducing existing power relations, or a tool of liberation.

Summary

This chapter considered how the interplay of writing and thinking is influenced by how writing is taught and learned. Tracing the debate between teaching writing as a product and teaching writing as a process, it revealed connections between standardized assessment, formulaic writing, and the writing experiences of teachers educated with and through these practices.

Multimodal approaches to writing, grounded in New Literacy Studies, offer a perspective of writing analogous to a process of design. This perspective enables writers to shape meaning freed from constraints of dominant modes or genres, creating opportunities for more diversity of language and thought. Because identities are socially constructed and fluid, empowering uses of language can facilitate the development of student agency by validating critical constructions of meaning. If, however, language is perceived primarily as a means of replicating authoritative views, if it is taught as a formulaic discipline to which only the privileged and educated have access, if it is assessed for form over content and facility with "old" printcentric conceptions of literacy, then students will learn that language is a weapon – a force to constrain them rather than an instrument of power to which they might gain access.

Extension Questions

1. Describe how writing as a product differs from writing as a process. How does each conception affect writing instruction? Create a metaphor or visual image that illustrates both conceptions of writing.
2. Write a narrative about your own experiences of writing and literacy practices. Reflect on and consider early childhood memories of writing and literacy, school experiences of literacy, and how home, school, and community writing are similar and different.
3. Explore how your identity as a writer may influence your role as a teacher of writing.
4. Discuss the role of emotion and cognition in composition. Create a writing prompt that integrates emotion and cognition and describe what you expect students would learn from writing a response to the prompt.
5. Explain how the idea of "design" relates to writing. What elements of design intersect with writing as a product and as a process?

Works Cited

Bartholomae, David, "Writing with Teachers: A Conversation with Peter Elbow." *College Composition and Communication*, vol. 46, no. 1, pp. 62–71, February 1995. www.jstor. org/stable/358870.

Dunn, Patricia A. "Does Bad 'Grammar' Instruction Make Writing Worse?" *Teachers, Profs, Parents: Writers Who Care*, January 2014. https://writerswhocare.wordpress.com/ 2014/01/27/does-bad-grammar-instruction-make-writing-worse/.

Gee, James Paul. *Social Linguistics and Literacies: Ideology in Discourses*. London, UK and New York, NY: Routledge, 1990.

Graves, Donald H. "Answering Your Questions About Teaching Writing: A Talk with Donald H. Graves." *Scholastic: Instructor*, 1995. www.scholastic.com/teachers/articles/tea ching-content/answering-your-questions-about-teaching-writing-talk-donald-h-graves/.

Kameen, Alex. "A Formula for Failure: The Problem with Formulaic Writing." *Teachers, Profs, Parents: Writers Who Care*, March 2017. https://writerswhocare.wordpress.com/ 2017/03/13/a-formula-for-failure-the-problem-with-formulaic-writing/.

Miller, Suzanne M. and Mary B. McVee, Editors. *Multimodal Composing in Classrooms: Learning and Teaching for the Digital World*. New York, NY and London, UK: Routledge, 2012.

Moffett, James. *Coming on Center: Essays in English Education*. Portsmouth, NH: Boynton/ Cook Publishers, 1988.

Murray, Donald. "Teach Writing as Process Not Product." *The Leaflet*, pp. 11–14, Fall 1972.

Ray, Katie Wood. *What You Know by Heart: How to Develop Curriculum for Your Writing Workshop*. Portsmouth, NH: Heinemann, 2002.

Schaffer, Jane C. *The Jane Schaffer Method: Teaching the Multiparagraph Essay: A Sequential Nine-Week Unit*. 3rd ed. San Diego, CA: Jane Schaffer Publications, 1995.

Smagorinsky, Peter. "Reason, Emotion, Thinking, and Writing in School." *Teachers, Profs, Parents: Writers Who Care*, August 2017. https://writerswhocare.wordpress.com/2017/ 08/21/reason-emotion-thinking-and-writing-in-school/.

Wood Ray, K. *What You Know by Heart: How to Develop Curriculum for Your Writing Workshop*. Portsmouth, NH: Heinemann, 2002.

6

THE POLITICS OF TEACHING

Are Teachers Agents of the State or Agents of Change?

The US presidential election was just days away and the whole school seemed energized. The race was close, and the candidates reflected views that were very different. At the October faculty meeting, the high school principal had cautioned teachers about being outspoken regarding the election. She expressed concerns about conflicts that might emerge, and potential bullying that could result from students who supported a less popular candidate.

Faculty who taught social studies disagreed about the principal's advice. Some felt that presenting a position of objectivity was appropriate, and they took pride in their students' inability to guess who they supported in the election. They believed that the teachers, despite their best efforts, always influenced students. Others felt that it was better to be direct, and to facilitate civil discussions so that students could experience how dissent is handled in a democracy. This group was convinced that teachers, whether or not they intended to, always provided clues that influenced students.

Most of the teachers in the English department were glad to avoid conversations about the election, and several were outspoken about their good fortune. Ebony, however, embraced the election as an opportunity to engage students in debates, analyze political rhetoric, and write persuasively for authentic audiences. As they walked toward the parking lot, Ebony's colleague and fellow English teacher, Andre, noted how fortunate she was to have avoided complaints from parents or students about the political content of her class.

"I'll bet you'll be glad to get back to teaching our regular curriculum after the election," Andre began. "No more worries about implicit, or explicit, messages in our lessons, right?"

Ebony stopped. "Are you kidding? It is a pleasure to have the politics out in the open, at least, instead of buried in a curriculum that pretends to be neutral and unbiased. Our hidden curriculum ignores the knowledge that our students bring to school, and it ignores the reality that our students are funded at half the rate of the school one town over. Our students are half as likely to graduate, and more likely to go to prison than to graduate from college. Ignoring those facts while we focus on teaching literary eras and semi-colons is a political stance, and it is one I can't take.

"Ebony," Andre replied, "you know that I am as committed to our students as you are, and I am fully aware of the challenges we face. Remember, I grew up here too. But if

we don't give students access to academic language, the ones who get to college will never succeed there."

"That may be true, but English class is just as political as social studies. How we teach reading, writing, speaking, and listening reflects our attitudes toward power and privilege in school, and in society. If we don't see our classrooms as political, if we pretend that language is neutral, then the best we can hope for is that a few of our students will assimilate. We will never effect real change. I expect more, and believe we can do better."

Introduction

Teaching, itself, is a political act. It involves decisions that have social and cultural implications, and these decisions are made and implemented in relation to different abilities to exercise power. Decisions about curriculum and instruction are not neutral; they support the status quo or they support change. As Turner explains:

> We are either recreating what is, conformity, or critically evaluating our world and knowledge, agency. Teaching a child to read and understand what the words mean is not neutral. Neither is teaching them how to phonetically sound out a word, but not how to understand its impact. Both are political acts; one supports independent thought and action, the other supports compliance.

Schools are sites where identities and social relations are shaped. Therefore, every interaction in school has the capacity to reinforce, or interrupt, existing power relations. As social institutions, schools reflect the values of the societies they serve. They also offer sites where change can occur. As mentioned in Chapter 1, schools – and the personnel who work within them – enact many purposes. They prepare students to live in contemporary society, and they prepare students to live in a world that might not yet be imagined. Schools sustain and perpetuate the existing social order, and they offer hope for a more equitable and just future. Educators may choose to perceive the work of education as apolitical, but that choice is a de facto selection of social reproduction. Teachers who see education as objective and politically neutral are, in reality, opting to replicate existing relations of power.

Exercises of power are embedded in social institutions. Because teaching occurs in social institutions, exercises of power are integrated in every interaction. Power is apparent in decisions about curriculum, including lessons and materials. Power is also revealed in how policies are developed and implemented, as well as in organizational structures. Since many of the activities around schooling involve language, it is important for English teachers to consider the political nature of teaching, as well as of language practices. In Chapter 1, large-scale and theoretical implications of power were discussed. In this chapter, the politics of school and classroom-level language will be explored. Contextual aspects of language with respect to power will be considered, as will some of the ways in which authority is enacted through positions and relationships. **High-stakes standardized assessments** will provide an illustration of how policy influences the lived experiences of teachers and students. The political role of teachers, as **public intellectuals** who can be **agents of the state** or **agents of change**, will be investigated, and the concept of **undisciplined English** as a means of integrating instrumental and exploratory purposes of schooling will be presented.

Teaching is Political

Whether or not it is acknowledged as such, teaching is inherently political. Sonia Nieto explains:

> Teaching is inherently political work. Although I do not mean to be unnecessarily provocative in making this assertion, after 40 years of teaching as both a K-12 teacher and, later, as a teacher educator, I have become convinced of the truth of this statement. Teaching is political in the sense that power and privilege – through decisions about funding, curriculum, class size, testing, tracking, and other matters of policy and practice – exacerbate rather than ease social class and race inequalities. In effect, then, education helps determine the life chances of young people based on their identities and zip codes. Teachers are an important part of this mix because what teachers say and do every day can have a tremendous impact on the lives of their students. (1)

Every interaction involves an exercise of power, and every interaction has the capacity to influence the life chances of students. This reality does not imply that teachers are autonomous, of course. Teachers do their work within the constraints of their positions, which tend to straddle lines of social class. The education level of teachers moves them toward middle-class status; however, the tightly scheduled nature of the daily work corresponds with working-class status. In addition, schools tend to be hierarchical institutions, with organizational charts reflecting direct lines of authority. This hierarchy is also evident in how state and federal regulations establish accountability systems. When such systems become familiar, they can be hard to notice and pay attention to because they seem natural and normal. They are, in a sense, embedded in the culture, and as such often go unquestioned. A critical perspective on education, however, questions assumptions around relations of power, building in opportunities to examine implications and consider alternatives. Investigating how decisions are made – including decisions about how authority is distributed and enacted – can begin by asking questions such as "who benefits?" and "who loses?" as a result of particular policies. It can be helpful to ask how curriculum and instruction, program offerings, assessment procedures, and discipline policies affect students, and whether the effects are reasonable and equitable. Similarly, it is important to examine the experiences of teachers, since their experiences impact students. As those closest to students, teachers are often most knowledgeable about institutional barriers to student success. If teachers have little voice in changing conditions, potential for change is reduced and students suffer. Further, classrooms tend to reflect the schools and systems in which they function.

This chapter will consider how schools reflect the politics of society, and how the politics of the classroom shape, and are shaped by, interactions among policy-makers, administrators, teachers, students, and members of the community. These interactions will be discussed using standardized assessments as an example of how policies intersect among various **stakeholders**. The chapter will conclude with an exploration of how the work of English teachers can transcend classroom walls and be a force for equity and justice.

Standardized Assessments

High-stakes testing often harms students' daily experience of learning, displaces more thoughtful and creative curriculum, diminishes the emotional well-being of educators and children, and unfairly damages the life-chances of members of vulnerable groups.

(NCTE)

High-stakes standardized assessments, defined as evaluative tools which have significant consequences for learners and sometimes teachers, are a key component of the contemporary **accountability movement** in education. The movement to standardize curriculum has grown and intensified through state initiatives and been reinforced by federal policies such as No Child Left Behind and Race to the Top. The accountability movement emphasizes standardized assessments as a means to ensure educational equity. Proponents of this approach to accountability define differential results in standardized assessment scores connected with gender, race, ethnicity, or other characteristics as "achievement gaps" that provide concrete evidence of inequities in the education system. Standardized assessments offer a way to identify these gaps, which is perceived as the first step toward addressing them. From this perspective, standardized assessments can reduce inequity by revealing gaps; they are a mechanism of objective accountability for schools, teachers, and learners.

Often, the ways of addressing what is termed the "achievement gap" involve instruction that resembles test preparation. This is a logical, predictable effect of test-based accountability systems. If student achievement is determined by a parti-cular assessment, then it makes sense to provide instruction that centers on the products related to that assessment. Unsurprisingly, this effect is typical and widely documented (Au; Dorn; Berliner).

Although many people, both inside and outside of the educational system, believe that standardized assessments are important for ensuring educational quality and equity, a critical look at standardized assessment raises many questions. One flaw in an accountability system based on standardized assessments is that it minimizes, or dismisses, the ways that standardized assessments serve to reproduce existing mechanisms of power and authority. High-stakes assessments are neither neutral nor objective. They are developed and implemented in ways that reinforce definitions of knowledge and skills that are valued. Furthermore, decades of research demonstrate that standardized assessment scores tend to correspond with factors that have less to do with student ability than they do with students' opportunity to learn.

In the US, public school funding is tied to property taxes. This means that educational resources are distributed unequally, with wealthier communities able to provide better schools with more highly qualified teachers, superior facilities, more challenging curricula, and a better selection of extracurricular activities. High-stakes standardized assessments have been shown to correspond primarily to the **socioeconomic status** of test takers. Further, they tend to advantage males over females, and certain racial and ethnic groups tend to perform better than others. In other words, one effect of standardized assessments is that, through the inherent cultural biases that privilege the knowledge and experiences of some groups over others, they produce evidence of an achievement gap that fortifies beliefs about students from different backgrounds. Beliefs about these gaps are then reinforced within the education system through instructional approaches that are reductive and alienating.

This matters because academic promotion and placement, as well as credentials such as high school diplomas, college admission, and financial aid, are frequently tied to standardized assessment scores. Consequently, young people's access to educational and career opportunities are closely intertwined with standardized assessments. High-stakes standardized assessments also affect how communities perceive students, how teachers perceive students, how students perceive themselves, and the language practices teachers and students experience in school.

High-stakes assessments influence perceptions of schools because student performance is aggregated, ranked, and publicized. Mass media outlets regularly report on school quality based primarily on student test scores. These reports rarely include information about the flaws in standardized assessments, about their historical use in supporting discrimination and oppression, and about how scores typically correspond with socioeconomic and cultural factors. Instead, some schools (usually well-funded and serving predominantly White students) compete for top spots in the rankings, while large urban schools are continually identified as failing. Consequences for failing schools can be severe, and often include threats of state takeover or "turnaround" plans that require replacement of teachers and administrators. Such punitive measures certainly harm teachers, but students suffer tremendous loss when their limited time in school is spent in underfunded schools with unqualified teachers. When schools are labeled as failing, they lose the most promising opportunity for improvement: more financial support.

Political leaders are reluctant to invest in poor schools, parents fear for their children's future and seek alternatives to local public schools, and this creates a cycle of failure, a self-fulfilling prophecy supported by an accountability system based on standardized assessments. Gunzenhauser asserts that the high-stakes accountability movement has redefined what it means to be an educated person (241). That is, intelligence is defined by standardized test scores. This redefinition, he notes, also displaces alternative modes of accountability, "such as community responsibility of equitable educational opportunities" (241).

High-stakes standardized assessments also affect the relationships between students and teachers. In part, this has to do with how teachers imagine and enact their roles. Teachers are **deprofessionalized** by an accountability movement that relies heavily on standardized assessments. Expectations are a politically dynamic factor in education. One way that high-stakes assessments deprofessionalize teachers is by restricting their ability to set and measure expectations. Dorn notes that recent reforms have shifted expectations from schools to students, further diminishing teachers' control. While schools have long been charged to encourage economic and social progress, the high-stakes testing movement, by using students' scores on standardized assessments as the basis for demonstrating achievement *and* earning credentials, sets the expectations for achievement explicitly on students. Using student test scores to assess accountability has significant consequences for teachers as well, a condition which Nichols and Berliner describe as unfair and unreasonable.

> Teachers are put in the precarious position of putting their livelihoods squarely on the shoulders of students. That is, unlike so many others whose work is evaluated based on their performance, teachers succeed or fail based on the performance of others! (150)

Teachers are disempowered by high-stakes assessments in two ways: First, expectations are standardized rather than dependent on their professional expertise; and second, teachers are held accountable for test scores which they, at best, co-construct with students (Nichols and Berliner). Under accountability systems in which expectations for learning and for writing are shaped by high-stakes tests, judgment based on professional dialogue is marginalized. This is problematic because effective education requires ongoing professional dialogue about purposes and expectations; high-stakes tests preclude such dialogue. Gunzenhauser emphasizes the significance of this development, stating that "high-stakes accountability has so dominated discourse and practices in public education that dialogue about the purpose and value of education has been circumscribed to dangerously narrow proportions" (242). The preclusion of professional dialogue is an effect of high-stakes testing which influences both the identities of teachers and the daily activities within classrooms.

Standardized assessments undermine the sense of autonomy which is a key aspect of teachers' professional identities. Instead of being the experts about their students' progress, standardized assessments capture, at best, a snapshot of student performance. This snapshot is made public, and becomes the basis for decisions about teacher and student achievement. In some cases, teachers' jobs and school survival are dependent on test scores. A related issue involves teacher perceptions of students. When teacher performance hinges on student test scores, teachers' ability to meet the needs of students is compromised. The purpose of education shifts from being answerable to a student and her community to being answerable to a technology of assessment – a single instrument that generates a numerical score. These conditions create ethical dilemmas for teachers, who must decide whether to focus on results that they deem inappropriate, or to risk their own positions as well as their students' access to opportunities or credentials. Teachers facing this dilemma may feel that must disavow their professional knowledge in order to pursue higher test scores for their classes (Taubman). These conditions create internal conflicts for teachers that can spill into teacher-student relationships. Teachers may be directed to focus instruction on students whose scores are more prone to improvement – that is, students whose scores are closer to the next higher set of benchmarks. For example, teachers might pay more attention to students whose scores are 60–64, knowing that they might be able to raise their scores to a 65 or above (often considered passing). They may also be encouraged to focus on students whose scores are 81–84, with the aim of achieving 85 (often considered mastery). These scenarios also imply that students whose scores are already below 60, above 85, or anywhere outside of the range of statistical significance on the assessment scale, receive less attention. It is conceivable that teachers could resent students whose scores could factor into teacher evaluations and school performance rankings. In these many ways, high-stakes tests and the curricula that support them affect the ways students and teachers define themselves, relate to one another, and experience schooling.

Literacy practices, as a component of culture, influence identity construction and social relations. Uses of language affect how students and teachers see themselves and behave toward one another. High-stakes standardized assessments have been demonstrated to shape curriculum and instruction, and their effects intensify in schools where the assessments reveal "achievement gaps." That is, students who attend schools in communities affected by poverty are more likely to experience instruction that is directly related to standardized assessments. Such instruction tends to be teacher-centered rather than student-centered, and oriented toward one-right-answer rather than inquiry-based. Since knowledge and skills tested on standardized assessments reflect academic literacies, language practices in poor and working-class communities are not likely to be present in test-based instruction, so students learn that their language is not valued. They learn that they are not readers or writers, and that their voices do not deserve to be amplified. Moreover, because many teachers attended public schools, their literacy identities have been shaped by high-stakes standardized assessments. The formative years of many of today's teachers have been profoundly influenced by the types of reading and writing required by these assessments. Unless explicitly challenged, the cycle of diminishing literacies will be perpetuated for generations.

Standardized assessments are an example of how power is exerted in educational settings. Because teachers and administrators regulate the **institutional mechanisms** necessary for students to earn the credentials for a diploma, students wishing to do so are always subjugated to their authority. Now, however, there are additional regulatory mechanisms related to high-stakes standardized assessments. In most public schools, both students and teachers are judged by student performance on these assessments, which are tightly controlled in administration and scoring. Assessments affect students directly because graduation is dependent on obtaining a passing-level performance. Assessments are used by administrators to tighten control of teachers because teachers are judged on the basis of their students' performance. State assessments, therefore, influence the actions of the administrators, who then increase their regulation of teachers. The regulation is direct in terms of the scoring, administration, and reporting procedures that teachers must adhere to. The regulation infiltrates the classroom when it involves submission of curricular materials and assessments that must show alignment with state assessments. The interactions described highlight the realities of shifting class relations within working-class schools. As public school teachers become increasingly subject to state control (through regulatory assessments), their role becomes more aligned with working-class norms. Although these conditions might seem to foster possibilities for *connecting* with their students, teachers increase control and regulation, resulting in increased alienation of students from teachers, from curriculum, and from their schools.

Standardized assessments offer a glimpse into the ways that policies influence schools, teachers, and students. As Saltman notes, the current **corporate reform movement** emphasizes education as apolitical. A corporate orientation toward education promotes the idea that content is neutral, and that its purpose is to prepare individuals as workers and consumers. Saltman explains:

> The now dominant business view of knowledge and teaching presumes that education is not inherently political, the principle educational problems involve methodological approaches to delivery of so-called content knowledge. Subjects such as English, math, science, and social studies in this view are seen as politically neutral or should be treated as politically neutral for students at most ages despite the fact that different individuals, cultural groups, and economic classes do not agree as to how these subjects should be taught or what counts as important to teach. (xv)

This vision of education may appear to resolve conflicts about the purposes of schools; however, these conflicts just become part of the hidden curriculum, rather than being openly discussed. Teachers, then, are faced with the challenge of handling conflicting purposes in ways that are answerable to learners and communities. To do this requires teachers to act as **public intellectuals**, to be both **agents of the state** and **agents of change**.

Agents of the State or Agents of Change

Teachers are charged to simultaneously enact the dual roles of "agent of the state" and "agent of change." As agents of the state, teachers are expected to maintain the status quo, serving current social needs and preparing students for today's world. As agents of change, teachers are expected to work with students and community members to construct a more equitable, just future. In general, there is greater institutional pressure to act as an agent of the state. Therefore, efforts to be agents of change require intentionality and commitment.

Factors that support the teachers, especially public school teachers, as agents of the state are powerful. First, public school teacher salaries are paid by tax dollars; teaching positions depend on the support of public funds. Salaries of educators in private settings often come from tuition or donors, and they are therefore subject to the demands of constituents, as well. Second, teaching licensure credentials, and the credentials educators confer upon students, are built on existing systems of knowledge and authority. Disrupting these systems can destabilize the authority on which the profession is built. Third, teachers serve as components of an education system that depends on us to fulfill numerous social contracts; society depends on educational institutions to produce qualified employees and professionals in many fields, including medicine, engineering, and law. Fourth, schools serve a custodial function, providing a space for youth to be safe and productive while the work of adults, such as sustaining systems related to government and commerce, continues. In these four ways, teachers maintain the status quo.

As agents of change, teachers also seek to support young people in the creation of a more just and equitable future. Teachers can do this in ways that protect both their integrity to their principles and their professional positions by cultivating critical dispositions that reflect the duality of their roles. They can examine the contexts in which they work and adopt perspectives consistent with the political nature of teaching. When teachers face dilemmas that seem to require them to disavow their professional knowledge, they may feel trapped between losing their integrity or losing their jobs. To counter this terrible choice, teachers might engage in an analysis of conflicting aspects of their practice using the frames of **critical compliance** and **reflective resistance**, discussed in Chapter 3. This first requires careful consideration of the conditions involved. Consistent with critical theoretical perspectives, teachers might explore how policies are developed, who benefits from their implementation, whose voices are present or absent, and the cultural and historical implications. The process of investigating the context may involve students and community members, and can be built into curriculum and instruction. When the analysis is complete, teachers can decide between the two paths of critical compliance and reflective resistance.

Critical compliance involves following mandates, but doing so while explicitly acknowledging their political origins and effects. Sometimes we must comply with policies even when we disagree with them, but this compliance does not require silence. We can comply and be publicly critical – even with our students. Other times, we may be able to resist, but with reflection – to ensure that our actions are aligned with our beliefs about teaching, learning, and learners. Selecting reflective resistance, a teacher would refuse to comply with policies that contradict her principles. Taking this approach reflectively, with collective support from colleagues and community members, can provide both advocacy and a measure of professional protection. Analyzing dilemmas with this duality reminds us that *every interaction among learners, teachers, and leaders has the potential to reproduce – or interrupt – structures of oppression.*

In the role of agent of change, teachers take on a critical perspective that connects to broader social issues. They might engage in credentialing activities, but consider, and publicize, how these perpetuate existing inequities. Working as an agent of change is often not perceived as what teachers should be paid, by the state, to do. By definition, agents of change aim to interrupt the status quo. Therefore, advocacy efforts related to acting as a change agent are treated more as an avocation than vocation.

The categories "agent of the state" and "agent of change" reveal how educators enact complex, sometimes contradictory, roles. To be an agent of the state is an institutional mandate. To be an agent of change is a moral imperative. In both roles, teachers can serve as public intellectuals.

Teachers as Public Intellectuals

Honoring the work of Edward Said, Greg Dimitriadis and Marc Lamont Hill identify three roles and responsibilities of public intellectuals:

1. They are experts in and contributors to their disciplines, and are responsible for passing along knowledge to future generations.
2. They must understand and participate in the broader social context. This may mean getting involved in policy discussions, writing letters to the editor, contributing voluntarily to support the field or the communities they serve.
3. While disciplinary expertise is essential, they must remain curious about domains outside of their discipline, to avoid becoming so narrowly focused as to be irrelevant.

The second responsibility, perhaps the most challenging, addresses accountability. It asks us to consider to whom, or to what, are teachers and schools accountable? We are also charged to define the "broader social context," and to explore what principles determine how teachers respond to "larger social and political issues"? These questions about accountability reaffirm the dichotomy of the roles of agent of the state and agent of change. Public intellectuals are accountable to society, to the people and the communities we serve. Regardless of political pressures, they are not accountable to policies or mandates that contradict the best interests of young people or their communities. Any definition of the "broader social context" that does not answer to people and communities is suspect, and public intellectuals should publicly subject it to rigorous inquiry. This stance is consistent with critical compliance and reflective resistance because both approaches involve dialogue and critique.

It is important to point out that the roles of agent of the state and agent of change only conflict when the aims of power contradict the needs and desires of the public. Change is necessary to combat injustice, so in a just society, change would not be required. Of course, a perfectly just and equitable society is aspirational, but this aspiration illuminates the significance of public intellectuals. In our imperfect society, the role of public intellectuals is to look for places where injustice exists, and to reveal its roots and its consequences. As public intellectuals, teachers can reflect on situations when being an agent of the state conflicts with their principles, and then address the gaps between the material realities and injustices of society, and the imagined realities of what could be.

In an ideal society, in a just society, there would be no gap between what is and what ought to be. In a just society, there would be no need for change. As long as a gap exists, public intellectuals are essential to identify and address inequities that challenge existing power relations. This chapter asks whether teachers are Agents of the State or Agents of Change, but as educators our charge is to shift the conjunction from "or" to "are." In a system that values justice, Agents of the State are Agents of Change. As agents of the state answerable to a more just tomorrow, we are obliged to be agents of change. As Martin Luther King famously claimed, "Injustice anywhere is a threat to justice everywhere." To combat injustice and uphold the principles of equity of opportunity that are central to democracy, teachers must work for change.

Undisciplining English Classrooms

Language, culture, and thought are deeply intertwined. What happens in English classrooms, then, has a great influence over student achievement. Although standards-based instruction and assessment currently dominate curriculum, English classrooms can provide leverage for learning that integrates excellence, equity, and opportunity.

One problem with standards-based education is that it contributes to fragmented learning experiences. Students tend to spend set periods of time in each of the content areas, and then move to the next, with little institutional support for making connections among disciplines. Content expertise can create silos that are detrimental to student learning. English teachers can intentionally cross boundaries by re-envisioning our work. We might question, in the critical theoretical tradition, our purposes, wondering, for example, whether it is our job to:

- Encourage students to reinforce boundaries, *or* break through them?
- Reproduce the status quo, *or* transform it?
- Prepare students for work in today's world, *or* position students to live in and to construct a world that we cannot yet imagine?

As discussed in Chapter 1, the role of teachers is related to the envisioned purposes of school. If the primary purpose of school is perceived as preparation for work, then education is **instrumental**. If the primary purpose of school is to promote inquiry and imagination, education is referred to as **exploratory**. Current educational policies emphasize the instrumental, focusing on evaluating educational effectiveness based on applicability to work, and even income. This orientation emphasizes the instrumental perspective, and minimizes the relevance of fields that are more exploratory in nature. Literature, classics, languages, and philosophy, for example, are being cut from colleges and universities as the value of degrees is being calculated on the basis of their **return on investment** in the world of work. While this determination should not be ignored, the educational worth cannot be reduced entirely to the predicted income of completers. Such an approach would support schools as places where inequities are reproduced rather than sites that promote movement toward justice.

Responses to attacks on liberal arts and humanities vary. Academics and educators can retrench in their disciplines, arguing for their relevance by demonstrating instrumental value in the workplace as well as social, human significance. This option allows teachers to maximize subject matter expertise, but forces students to make conceptual, intellectual leaps between disciplines. Educators might instead reach outside their disciplines to create **contingent collaborations** that represent superficial efforts toward **interdisciplinarity**. A third approach, and one that is particularly suited for English classrooms, involves reaching beyond disciplinary silos to create fields of practice that reject the false dichotomy of exploratory versus instrumental. An "**undisciplined**" perspective that unites instrumental and exploratory approaches creates an environment for our field to survive, but, even more importantly, for our learners to thrive.

Disciplines are generally understood as branches of knowledge. To develop disciplinary expertise requires training "in a system of orderly behavior recognized as characteristic of the discipline" (Del Favero). This training is a form of socialization and acculturation, since it involves adopting and applying particular ways of thinking and being. In essence, "disciplinary worlds are considered separate and distinct cultures that exert varying influence on scholarly behaviors as well as on the structure of higher education" (Del Favero). The word "discipline" is rooted in the term "disciple," or pupil, but also evokes control and compliance with rules and norms.

In our educational, vocational, avocational, and recreational lives, we become acculturated into disciplines. We learn to use vocabulary associated with discourses to meet certain expectations and to follow rules of behavior. Disciplinary training can provide guideposts and handrails that help develop deep knowledge – and even allow us to stretch disciplinary boundaries. But disciplines are also silos that keep scholars separate, speaking other languages encoded in unfamiliar lexicons. Most importantly, disciplines can create barriers to diverse perspectives. Like all big concepts, disciplines present challenges and opportunities that lend themselves to critical questions: How can we grow, and grow within our discipline, while we traverse its boundaries? How can we create opportunities for students to develop critical literacies for the existing world and simultaneously support literacies that create a more just and beautiful world?

From a traditional perspective, disciplines are branches of knowledge. These branches might sprout leaves that interconnect, but the connections are ultimately unsupported – leaves entangling in the air. English teachers can modify this metaphor, and work to ensure that disciplines serve as interconnected roots from which students can grow new knowledge. If disciplines are envisioned as roots, bonds among disciplines grow naturally and are mutually strengthening. Rather than interdisciplinary literacy, I refer to this as "**undisciplined English**." The trouble with English instruction that is interdisciplinary is that it exists in spaces between disciplinary silos. Interdisciplinary language instruction, therefore, tends to have flexibility but lack support. Limbs and leaves between these silos may be promising and original, but they are also isolated and vulnerable. Undisciplined English is rooted in disciplinary knowledge, but intentionally cultivates **critical dispositions** toward learning through projects and assessments that are authentic and relevant to the lives of learners.

Critical dispositions involve questioning what constitutes knowledge and how expertise is developed and determined. This ongoing analysis, which is inclusive of individuals and contexts and interrelations of power, addresses the dual purposes of instrumental and exploratory purposes of education. Critical dispositions involve:

- An orientation toward ongoing engagement and struggle rather than a problem/solution approach to education. It is in areas of tension where meaningful learning occurs, and where critical reflection is most necessary. Rather than seeing achievement gaps as hollows to be filled in, critical dispositions encourage educators to plunge with their students into difficult issues with empathy, wisdom, and openness. This approach facilitates professional growth and models thoughtful, productive dialogue.
- Appreciation of the significance of genuine, **dialogic relationships**, teaching and learning. Dialogic relationships emerge when the voices of all participants are heard and valued, allowing for authentic dialogue to generate knowledge and understanding. Such relationships create learning environments where questions are central.

- Preference for questions over answers and inquiry over facts. Questioning why things are the way they are often generates additional questions. Focusing on the process of inquiry creates instructional activities that are fundamentally different from fact-based teaching that emphasizes recitation or memorization. Curriculum constructed on questions supports the development of critical dispositions in teachers and students.
- Understanding that teachers are preparing learners to construct a world that does not yet exist. Critical dispositions allow space for information, as well as for imagination, thus integrating instrumental and exploratory perspectives.
- Awareness that educators make countless decisions in myriad, ever-changing contexts, and that the results of these decisions are often unpredictable and immeasurable. Critical dispositions reinforce professional autonomy by privileging professional judgment and creating a strong foundation for teacher autonomy grounded in answerability to youth and their communities.

Teachers and students can practice critical dispositions to question norms and interrogate the curriculum. Examples of questions that might guide curriculum to support critical dispositions are:

- What are the purposes for reading and writing, and how do these purposes transcend the classroom?
- What texts are read and written as part of the curriculum? What texts are missing?
- How do relations of power and privilege influence how literacies are taught and learned? Consider current conditions and policies and find out who decides? Who benefits? Who loses?

Undisciplined English make academic, disciplinary norms visible and explicit to ensure that diverse language practices are valued. Teachers create opportunities for students' home and community language practices to be used in school and applied in authentic products by designing experiences for students to explore how to make meaning in ways that both employ and defy disciplinary conventions (see Box 6.1). This involves co-constructing, with students and colleagues, authentic projects in which students can use skills and apply content while cultivating critical dispositions that reveal and challenge existing power relations. As Gorski notes, "There is no path to justice that does not involve a direct confrontation with injustice." To further support undisciplined English and the development of critical dispositions, teachers can provide possibilities for students to demonstrate knowledge and skills to different audiences through a variety of modes. Ultimately, undisciplined English involves integrating exploratory and instrumental purposes so that students can thrive in today's world while imagining and constructing a better tomorrow.

BOX 6.1 UNDISCIPLINED ENGLISH: EXAMPLES FROM THE FIELD

Connecting Past and Present: A Local Research Project

Created by Linda Templeton
Published by NCTE readwritethink
www.readwritethink.org/classroom-resources/lesson-plans/connecting-past-p resent-local-1027.html?tab=1#tabs

When students make real-world connections between themselves and their community, they can participate in authentic communication activities based on issues that matter to them personally. In this activity, students research a decade in their school's history, with small groups researching specific topics. This lesson plan was developed as part of a collaborative professional writing initiative sponsored by the Kennesaw Mountain Writing Project (KMWP) at Kennesaw State University.

Just Science

Written by Darlene Koenig
Published by Teaching Tolerance
www.tolerance.org/magazine/summer-2013/just-science

Teachers share examples that bring literacy and social justice into the science lab, providing lessons that link critical literacy, a sense of place, and authentic artifacts.

Where I'm From

Published by George Ella Lyon, Writer and Teacher
www.georgeellalyon.com/where.html

As Kentucky's 2015–2016 poet laureate, George Ella wants to collect a "Where I'm From" poem from every county in Kentucky. Kentucky's "'Where I'm From': A Poetry of Place" is the central theme of a project that will touch all 120 of Kentucky's counties. Find more information, and how to submit poems, on the Kentucky Arts Council website.

Young Voices for the Planet

Published by Young Voices for the Planet
www.youngvoicesonclimatechange.com/

The mission of the *Young Voices for the Planet* film series is to limit the magnitude of climate change and its impacts by empowering children and youth, through uplifting and inspiring success stories, to take an essential role in informing their communities – and society at large, challenging decision-makers, and catalyzing change.

Summary

This chapter examined teaching as a political act and curricula as sets of decisions that are exercises of power. Schools, as social institutions, influence the identities of students and can reinforce or interrupt relations of power. How policies intersect in the daily lives of students and teachers was explored through the example of high-stakes standardized assessments, which shape how literacy practices are taught, learned, and evaluated in schools. As mechanisms of the accountability movement, standardized assessments purport to promote equity and excellence by revealing achievement gaps. However, high-stakes standardized assessments have especially negative effects on historically marginalized learners and tend to reinforce existing relations of power. High-stakes standardized tests affect how students and teachers perceive themselves and how they relate to one another. They also influence whether language is experienced as a weapon of oppression or a tool for transformation.

Since teaching is inherently political, consideration of the role of teachers is vital. This chapter discussed teachers as public intellectuals who can be agents of the state or agents of change. To handle the dilemmas created by the conflicts in these roles, teachers, as public intellectuals, can use the frames of critical compliance and reflective resistance.

Finally, returning to the purposes of education as instrumental or exploratory, this chapter presented undisciplined English. Reimagining disciplines as roots rather than branches, undisciplined English cultivates critical dispositions and can contribute to integrating instrumental and exploratory aims in ways that are answerable to learners and their communities.

Extension Questions

1. Many teacher education programs focus on professional dispositions. Locate documents related to professional dispositions in one or more programs and analyze them. What characteristics are featured? Are dispositions taught as part of the program, or are they just assessed? What changes would you recommend?
2. Reflect on your own experiences of education and identify an example of a professional dilemma. Explain how this dilemma might be approached through critical compliance and reflective resistance.
3. Review examples of instructional plans in Box 6.1. Identify the characteristics that are consistent with the five tenets that support critical dispositions (pp. 95–96).
4. All policy initiatives have intended and unintended consequences. Identify an example of an educational policy and examine effects of that policy on teachers and learners. Consider the origins and aims of the policy and the short- and long-term consequences of implementation.

5.   English education, as a discipline, has a long history. What components of English as an academic discipline are essential? How can English teachers support academic collaborations that draw on undisciplined English?

Works Cited

Au, Wayne. "Social Studies, Social Justice: W(h)ither the Social Studies in High-Stakes Testing?" *Teacher Education Quarterly*, vol. 36, no. 1, 2009.

Berliner, David C. *Poverty and Potential: Out-of-School Factors and School Success.* Education Policy Research Unit, 2009. http://nepc.colorado.edu/publication/poverty-and-potential.

Del Favero, Marietta. "Academic Disciplines – Disciplines and the Structure of Higher Education, Discipline Classification Systems, Discipline Differences." http://education.stateuniversity.com/pages/1723/Academic-Disciplines.html.

Dimitriadis, Greg and Marc LamontHill. "Accountability and the Contemporary Intellectual." *Bank Street Occasional Paper Series*, no. 27, 2012. www.bankstreet.edu/scholarly-initiatives/occasional-paper-series/27/part-i/accountability-and-contemporary-intellectual/.

Dorn, Sherman. *Accountability Frankenstein: Understanding and Taming the Monster.* Charlotte, NC: Information Age Publishing, 2007.

Gorski, Paul. *Twitter* thread of August 24, 2017. https://twitter.com/pgorski/status/900898326039719936.

Gunzenhauser, Michael G. "Normalizing the Educated Subject: A Foucaultian Analysis of High-Stakes Accountability." *Educational Studies*, vol. 39, no. 3, pp. 241–259, 2006.

National Council of Teachers of English. *Resolution on Urging Reconsideration of High Stakes Testing.* November 2000. www2.ncte.org/statement/highstakestestrecons/.

Nichols, Sharon L. and David C. Berliner. *Collateral Damage: How High-Stakes Testing Corrupts America's Schools.* Cambridge, MA: Harvard Education Press, 2007.

Nieto, Sonia. "Teaching as Political Work: Learning from Courageous and Caring Teachers." Bronxville, NY: Sarah Lawrence College, Child Development Institute, Spring 2006.

Said, Edward. *Representations of the Intellectual.* New York, NY: Vintage Books, 1994.

Saltman, Kenneth J. "Corporate Schooling Meets Corporate Media: Standards, Testing, and Technophilia." *Review of Education, Pedagogy, and Cultural Studies*, vol. 38, no. 2, pp. 105–123, April 2016.

Taubman, Peter. "Educational Revolution." *Bank Street Occasional Paper Series*, no. 27, pp. 14–17, 2012.

Templeton, Linda. "Connecting Past and Present: A Local Research Project." *ILA/NCTE*, 2017. www.readwritethink.org/classroom-resources/lesson-plans/connecting-past-present-local-1027.html.

Turner, Jane. "Teaching is a Political Act." *Teacher Newsmagazine*, vol. 23, no. 2, October 2010. https://bctf.ca/publications/NewsmagArticle.aspx?id=21678.

APPENDIX A: USING THE EXPAND FRAMEWORK TO FOSTER CRITICAL REFLECTION

The introductory scenarios at the start of each chapter are intentionally crafted to be engaging narratives that raise complex, multifaceted questions. The EXPAND analytical framework aims to enrich and improve the effectiveness of the scenarios by facilitating dialogue and fostering critical reflection. This process is intended to extend understanding and to enhance appreciation of the complexities that underlie every aspect of education.

Directions:

1. Read the scenario.
2. After reading the case story, use the analytical framework below to *expand* the concepts and issues involved.

TABLE A.1 The EXPAND Analytical Framework

E X P A N D	Phase of the EXPAND Process	Application to the Scenario
EX	Explain the problem. Briefly state the issues involved, particularly as they relate to teaching and learning. How does the scenario connect to the concepts raised in the chapter? Describe the dilemma in the context of research on related topics.	
PERSPECTIVES	Identify what you think are the perspectives of participants in the scenario. What do the perspectives have in common? In what ways do they differ or conflict?	
ASSUMPTIONS	An *assumption* is a belief that is taken for granted. Discuss the beliefs, attitudes, or values that might underlie the perspectives of participants. What experiences make them think and act the way they do? What legal, theoretical, cultural, and/or ethical underpinnings support participants' perspectives? What stereotypes are being perpetuated or challenged?	
NOT THERE	What important information is missing from the scenario? What do you wish you knew? What questions would you ask people involved in the scenario? What documents would you like to have access to? How might the omitted information affect the analysis? If the information were provided, how might the analysis change?	
DO NEXT	In order to address issues raised in the case scenario, what should the next steps be?	

Adapted from Julie A. Gorlewski and David Gorlewski. *Making it Real: Case Stories for Secondary Students.* Boston, MA: Sense Publishing, Inc., 2012.

APPENDIX B: GLOSSARY OF KEY TERMS

1 **3D printing** is the process of creating a three-dimensional physical object from a digital file. In composition, a design approach to instruction can draw on the concept of 3D printing by creating possibilities for original formatting options.

2 **Academic disciplines** are fields of study defined by specific vocabularies, ways of thinking, and categories of what counts as evidence and knowledge. In schools, academic disciplines generally include English language arts, social studies, sciences (such as biology, chemistry, physics, and earth science), and mathematics. Additional academic disciplines are performing arts, philosophy, and engineering, among others.

3 **Academic literacy** refers to the skills necessary to read, write, speak, and listen in ways that are valued in educational institutions. Academic literacies become more specific as a learner progresses in various disciplines, requiring proficiency in composition, vocabulary, oral, and auditory abilities.

4 **Accountability**, or the **accountability movement** in education, experienced a resurgence in the mid-1990s. Generally connected to standards-based assessment systems, accountability in this context involves ranking student, teacher, and school performance on the basis of high-stakes standardized tests.

5 The **achievement gap** is the difference on standardized assessment results among different groups of students. Achievement gaps are constructed on the assumption that standardized assessments are an objective measure of student achievement. However, standardized assessments have been demonstrated to yield results that correspond to wealth and privilege, and the achievement gap fails to take this into consideration. Furthermore, differences in school funding and educational resources contribute to

disparities in assessment results, so the achievement gap primarily serves to reinforce stereotypes about children of color, as well as children whose communities are marked by poverty.

6 **Aesthetics**, in relation to literary criticism, evaluates a work primarily on the basis of beauty. Beauty is valued over meaning and over socio-political relevance. A concern about aesthetics is that what is beautiful tends to be determined on the basis of existing social capital, so those already having power are most able to decide what aesthetics are elite and most esteemed.

7 **Agents of change** are people who intend to effect transformation in an organization or a society. Change agents look for opportunities to create leverage in order to make significant and often sweeping shifts in policy and behavior.

8 **Agents of the state** hold positions in the public sphere that require them to uphold existing policies and procedures. Generally paid by public funds, such as tax revenue, agents of the state have a fiduciary responsibility to the government.

9 **Answerability**, in contrast to accountability, requires educators to be responsible to learners and their communities. Answerability in education is not limited to classrooms and schools; it also shapes educational research by compelling scholars to articulate how studies are inclusive and responsible to all participants.

10 An **artifact** is a concrete representation of a culture, concept, or idea. Texts are artifacts or language, which can also be perceived as an artifact of culture. Because artifacts are concrete, they exist across time and can be interpreted both in light of the eras of their origin, as well as in contemporary contexts.

11 **Aspirational standards** are an ideal, a goal toward which people constantly strive. In education, aspirational standards include equity, excellence, and inclusivity. In all these areas, separately and in combination, ongoing examination of policies and practices will reveal areas where improvement is necessary. For example, increasing expectations for excellence might create challenges related to equity and inclusivity. Aspirational standards are intended to promote continuous improvement.

12 **Assessment**, broadly defined, refers to evaluation of learning. Assessment instruments can be local and teacher-based, school wide, or standardized. Research shows that assessment tends to drive instruction; that is, learning experiences are often developed with the student performance on assessments in mind. Therefore, assessments that focus on knowledge of facts promote lessons geared toward repetition of information. On the other hand, assessments that involve application and construction of knowledge tend to encourage inquiry-based instruction.

13 **Assumptions** are deeply held and often unexamined beliefs, typically established within cultural norms and experiences. Unexamined

assumptions affect teacher and student attitudes toward learning and toward one another, and can contribute to expectations for learners that are related to stereotypes.

14   The **banking model**, or **transmission model**, of education is attributed to educational scholar and activist Paolo Freire. In this conception of education, learners are perceived as "blank slates" or "empty vessels" and the role of teachers is to transmit existing knowledge to students. This model of education presents education as a passive experience of replicating authoritative knowledge.

15   In the field of writing instruction, Bartholomae describes **basic writers** as those who have not yet developed competence in academic discourse. According to Bartholomae, this lack of proficiency creates barriers for basic writers to compose with the authority necessary to be taken seriously by readers. Rather than focusing on the convention of correcting errors, Bartholomae posits that basic writers need to develop fluency in academic discourse by mimicking writing practices in the academic community.

16   **Close reading**, grounded in a New Critical literary theory, emphasizes texts as freestanding artifacts of meaning and represents a text-centered theory of literature. Applying a close reading approach involves decoding and analyzing texts to gain comprehension.

17   The **College Board** is a not-for-profit organization, founded in 1900, that is composed of a membership of more than 6,000 institutions of education. The organization collects and distributes data about students in secondary schools and higher education, administers and scores assessments such as the SAT, and oversees the Advanced Placement Program, which allows high school students to earn college credit. Through its many programs and services, including achievement and aptitude tests, the College Board is a powerful influence on how college readiness is evaluated.

18   **Colonialism** is the exploitation of people and resources to benefit colonizers. On a global scale, this involves appropriating land and resources by creating a colony that is occupied and controlled by the oppressor. Colonialism also involves enslavement of people and exploiting their bodies and labor in ways that create profit for colonizers. Colonialism is a system of exploitation that supports violence against and erasure of people, their lands, and their cultures.

19   An outgrowth of the standards and accountability movement, the **Common Core Standards**, were developed through an initiative begun in 2009 and led by the Council of Chief State School Officers (CCSSO) and the National Governors Association Center for Best Practices (NGA Center). Focused on what students need to know and be able to do in the areas of English language arts/literacy and mathematics, the Common Core Standards sought to create consistent expectations for learning. They were adopted by over 40 states, in part because their implementation was heavily incentivized by funding tied to federal Race to the Top legislation. Their use has been controversial, especially when the standards were associated with high-stakes assessments, and some states have reverted to local curriculum standards.

20 **Communities of practice**, in relation to literacy, refer to cultural systems of communication involving shared discourse. A community of practice might be circumscribed by geographic boundaries, by professional preparation and performance, and by participation in avocational or recreational activities. Discursive practices related to a community of practice include a shared lexicon, common modes of expression, and collective understandings of how texts are consumed and produced.

21 Derived from the Latin "componere," which means "put together," **composition** in the field of English is associated with writing. Authors and developing writers alike engage in the act of composing, or putting together ideas in texts meant to be published for particular audiences or readers. A composition is the artifact that results from this act of composing.

22 **Constructivist/constructivism,** as a paradigm or worldview, posits that learning is an active, constructive process in which the learner is the information constructor. Students actively construct their own representations of objective reality as new information is linked to *prior knowledge*. Constructivism is a reaction to more didactic approaches such as behaviorism and programmed instruction. A constructivist views the learner not as a blank slate (tabula rasa) but as one who brings past experiences and cultural factors to a learning situation. Famous constructivists include L.S. Vygotsky, and J. Piaget.

23 In relation to literacy, people **consume** various types and modes of texts when they make meanings with and through them. Consuming texts can be perceived as an active process in which meanings are constructed, or a passive process that involves decoding prescribed meanings.

24 **Content standards**, formerly called Subject Area Standards, refer to a defined domain of knowledge and skills in an academic program. The most common content areas in public schools are English language arts, mathematics, science, and social studies. Content standards are broad statements that describe *specific content* that groups of students should learn at *each grade level*. In English language arts, content standards address the sub-skills of reading, writing, listening, and speaking. In addition to the Common Core State Standards, various states and professional organizations (such as the National Council of Teachers of English) have developed their own sets of content standards. The commonality between and among these content standards lies in the scaffolding of skills as students move from one grade to the next. For example, the standard for 9th and 10th grade students under the heading of "argumentative writing" may include five specific

characteristics (such as "establish and maintain a formal tone") while the standard for eleventh and twelfth graders would include the same five characteristics with the *addition* of a sixth characteristic (such as "use specific rhetorical devices to support assertions"). Content standards, in and of themselves, are generally not seen as problematic. The criticism lies in the use of standardized testing of those standards to evaluate teachers, administrators, schools, and school districts when childhood poverty is arguably the main reason for poor student performance.

25 Based on the work of Tuck and Yang, contingent **collaborations** refer to associations based on common goals that recognize that partners in collaborations are differently implicated and affected by relations of power and privilege. Endeavors formed as contingent collaborations are distinct from those grounded in aims of solidarity, which often disregard differences among collaborators.

26 The **corporate reform movement**, in large part, is funded by major foundations, Wall Street hedge fund managers, entrepreneurs, and the US Department of Education. The term *corporate reform* is a political one; and Cuban argues that it is a mistake to overstate the homogeneity of the corporate reformers' perspectives and purposes. The power players in this movement, he contends, have "varied, not uniform motives." Cuban argues that there are two different senses of the term. The first is that corporate reform is a movement led by corporate elites – often with different goals. The second is that corporate reform is a movement to remake public education in the image and likeness of for-profit corporations in a competitive marketplace.

27 **Critical compliance**, coupled with reflective resistance, provides pathways for educators to enact a critical perspective without sacrificing access to social and cultural capital, such as credentials. A teacher taking a stance of critical compliance would fulfill requirements of policy mandates, but would also critique features that contribute to inequity.

28 **Critical disability studies (CDS)** considers how institutions, cities, or societies "dis-able" people systemically and socially as well as looking at how the body and impairment can critically be incorporated into the discussions of disability and disablement. Disabilities studies emerged from the disabilities rights movement. Critical disabilities studies also examine how disability intersects with race, gender, class, and sexuality in ways that influence wider power relations and personal experience.

29 **Critical dispositions** are a set of critical thinking skills such as analysis, evaluation, and inference connected to a variety of personal dispositions such as open-mindedness, inquisitiveness, and skepticism. To have a critical disposition is the ability and desire to e.g., try to be well-informed, take into account the total situation, look for alternatives, take a position (and change a position) when the evidence is sufficient to do so, and be sensitive to the feelings, level of knowledge, and degree of sophistication of others.

30   **Critical literacy** is the ability to read text in a manner that promotes a deeper understanding of socially constructed concepts such as power, inequality, and injustice in human relationships. Critical literacy encourages individuals to question the attitudes, values and beliefs of written texts, visual applications, and spoken words. Facilitating the development of critical literacy advances the examination and reform of social situations and exposes students to the hidden agendas within texts.

31   **Critical pedagogy** is a teaching method that challenges any form of social oppression and its related customs and beliefs. A critical pedagogical approach enables students to gain a critical awareness, criticize the established order, and question society in its understanding of the role of education. From this point of view, social critique is necessary if one does not want an education that reproduces the status quo. Key concepts of critical pedagogy are emancipation and liberation from oppressive social relations, as well as the cultivation of the intellect. Paolo Freire, considered a major contributor to critical pedagogy, elaborates on critical pedagogy in his book *Pedagogy of the Oppressed*.

32   **Critical race theory** (CRT) was originally used as an analytical framework to assess inequity in education (Decuir and Dixson). The term CRT stems from the field of critical legal studies, which addresses the racial inequities in society. The main goal of critical race theorists is to expose hidden systemic and customary ways in which racism works by drawing from a wide range of sources of knowledge that range from statistics to social science research to personal experience. Critical race theorists have elaborated on the following: the centrality of racism; challenges to claims of neutrality, color blindness, and meritocracy; whites as beneficiaries of racial remedies; centrality of experiential knowledge; and commitment to working for social justice.

33   **Critical theory** involves the systematic, intentional questioning of relations of power. Critical theory interrogates how categories of knowledge, including language, are constructed, produced, and reproduced. A critical approach to education aims to reveal injustices. Because it exposes institutional inequities, and schools are institutions, critical education jeopardizes the established existence of the organizations through which it occurs. By raising questions that lead to action, critical education represents change.

34   **Cultural capital** consists of the social assets of a person – such as the level of education, intellect, and style of speech and dress, etc. that, in effect, work to promote social mobility. According to Bourdieu, cultural capital falls into three categories: institutionalized (education or specialized knowledge), embodied (personality, speech), and objectified (clothes or other possessions). Cultural capital is used to reinforce class differences as groups of people have differing sources and forms of knowledge depending on variables such as race, class, gender, ethnicity, nationality, religion, and even age.

35   **Cultural practices** involve rituals and daily activities related to family and institutional life. Generally perceived as part of the fabric of ordinary life, cultural practices tend to be unquestioned. In and of themselves, cultural practices are free from value or status; however, value and status are ascribed in accordance to relations of power and privilege in society (see **cultural capital**).

36   **Culturally relevant pedagogies**, also referred to as *culturally responsive teaching*, are grounded in teachers displaying cultural competence, i.e., skill at teaching in a cross-cultural or multicultural setting. According to Ladson-Billings, the teacher displays this "competence" by enabling each student to relate course content to his or her cultural context.

37   **Culturally responsive pedagogies** represent a student-centered approach to teaching in which the student's unique strengths are identified and nurtured to promote student achievement and a sense of well-being about the student's place in the world. The culturally responsive teacher uses the students' backgrounds, social experiences, prior knowledge, and learning styles to enhance the teaching/learning process.

38   **Culturally sustaining pedagogies** (CSP) seek to *perpetuate and foster* linguistic, literate, and cultural pluralism as part of schooling for positive social transformation. CSP explicitly call for schooling to be a site for sustaining – rather than eradicating – the cultural ways of communities of color. Under CSP, a student's cultural background is viewed as an asset to be nourished, not as a deficit.

39   **Curriculum** generally refers to 1) all the courses offered by an educational institution (the *high school curriculum*) or 2) a set of courses constituting an area of specialization (the *English language arts curriculum*). These definitions view curriculum as a tangible entity manifesting itself *explicitly* as a formal booklet or guide listing the content standards for a program or course (also called the Explicit, Overt, Formal, or Written Curriculum). Less tangible are various curriculum types including, but not limited to, the Hidden Curriculum, the Null Curriculum, the Delivered Curriculum, and the Received Curriculum – all defined in this Glossary.

40   **Curriculum mapping** is the process of indexing or diagramming a curriculum to identify and address academic gaps, redundancies, and misalignments for the purposes of improving the overall coherence of a course of study and, by extension, its effectiveness. Curricula may be mapped vertically or horizontally. Vertical alignment focuses on the content and skills being taught from one grade level to the next (for example, looking for gaps or redundancies in writing instruction from grades 6 through 12) while horizontal alignment would analyze content skills across a grade level (for example, looking for gaps and redundancies in teaching literature across all grade 9 teachers in a school or school district).

41   The **delivered curriculum** represents the elements of the Explicit/Written/ Overt Curriculum that the teacher presents to the students. The explicit

curriculum becomes the delivered curriculum when it is enacted through classroom practice. When learners experience curriculum and construct knowledge in relation to their own lives, the delivered curriculum becomes the received curriculum.

42 In the current educational climate which is connected closely to the corporate reform movement, teachers are becoming **de-professionalized**. That is, decisions that teachers typically made in the past such as selecting materials, employing a range of methodologies, assessing and evaluating students, writing curriculum, and determining if a student has passed a course of study (decisions requiring professional expertise) have been increasingly centralized. De-professionalization in education is characterized by increased standardized testing of students, over-reliance on standardized test results, mandated programmed instruction, and adherence to prescribed curricula – often developed by private, for-profit corporations. Additionally, student achievement on standardized tests is often linked to teacher, administrator, and school/school district evaluations.

43 In the context of writing and writing instruction, **design** extends under-standings of "composition," to evoke innovation in form and function. Thinking about making meaning as a process of design opens space for reimagining modes of writing, emphasizing innovation and possibility over competence and conventions. The metaphor of writing as design intends to be more inclusive of diverse voices, cultures, and literacy practices.

44 **Dialogic relationships** are the result of egalitarian dialogue; the con-sequence of a dialogue in which people provide arguments based on validity claims and not on power claims. Ideally, the dialogic relationship results in *dialogic learning*. The concept of dialogic learning is frequently linked to the Socratic dialogues in which knowledge is constructed through discussion.

45 **Digital discourse** involves information technologies and the Internet. It is also defined as the *set of competencies* for full participation in a knowledge society involving the effective use of digital devices such as smartphones, tablets, laptops, and desktop PCs for purposes of communication, expression, collaboration, and advocacy.

46 **Digital video** is a representation of moving visual images in the form of encoded digital data. This differs from analog video, which represents moving visual images with analog signals. When copied, analog video experiences generation loss (that is, each copy is of reduced quality); digital video does not.

47 The term **discourse** refers to intersections among language, culture, and identity. As social constructions, discourses are modes of communication that shape, and are shaped by, relations of power. Discourses affect how people think and behave. As linguistic forces that operate through everyday cultural activities, discourses emerge from and influence ideologies, insti-tutions, categories of knowledge, and interactions among individuals and groups of people.

48 **Dispositions** are a person's inherent qualities of mind and character; and are related to one's temperament, nature, make-up, and mentality. Having *critical* dispositions (see #29) implies that an individual, as an inherent quality, takes a critical stance by habitually questioning prevailing attitudes, beliefs, and practices; in short, questioning the status quo.

49 **English language arts** is the study and improvement of the arts of language; in this context, the English language, through the skills of reading, writing, listening, and speaking. There has been much debate about the role of English language arts as a stand-alone core academic subject as opposed to a subject in service of all other subjects (a more utilitarian perspective).

50 **Epistemology** is the branch of philosophy concerned with the theory of knowledge. Epistemology studies the nature of knowledge, justification, and the rationality of belief, as well as the origin, methods, and limits of human knowledge.

51 **Explicit curriculum** (see also formal curriculum or written curriculum) is that which is written as part of formal instruction in a school. It may refer to a curriculum *document*, texts, and other supportive materials that are *overtly chosen* to support the intentional instructional agenda of a school.

52 In contrast to an instrumental perspective of education, an **exploratory** approach emphasizes process and imagination over behavioral objectives and prescriptive instructional experiences. Exploratory purposes of school focus less on job preparation and more on the development of intellect, analytical abilities, and human talent.

53 **Expressive skills** include facial expressions, gestures, intentionality, vocabulary, semantics, morphology, and syntax (grammar rules). To use *expressive language* means being able to put thoughts into words and sentences in a way that makes sense and is grammatically accurate.

54 **Extra curriculum (extra–curricular)** consists of any activities or programs that fall outside the realm of the normal school academic curriculum. In schools, activities outside the regular formal curriculum generally include sports teams, clubs, or organizations (such as the Student Council, Orchestra, or the National Honor Society).

55 **Feminist theory** is an extension of feminism into theoretical, fictional, or philosophical discourse. It aims to understand the nature of gender inequality and examines women's and men's social roles, experiences, interests, chores, and politics in a variety of fields, such as anthropology and sociology. Feminist theory is distinctive for how its creators shift their analytic lens, assumptions, and topical focus away from the male viewpoint and experience. In doing so, feminist theory shines light on social problems, trends, and issues that are often overlooked or misidentified by the historically dominant male perspective within social theory.

56 In writing instruction, **form** refers to the genre or mode of the written product. Examples of forms include a five-paragraph essay, a Shakespearean sonnet, or any type of writing in which the structure is formulaic. A perpetual tension in the field involves whether, and to what extent, form should be privileged over function.

57   **Formal curriculum**, also referred to as the Explicit, Overt, or Written curriculum, is the curriculum developed, adopted, and officially sanctioned by a school or school district. The Formal curriculum generally lists the content, skills, and dispositions for each grade level and each subject area.

58   **Formulaic writing,** as opposed to *authentic writing*, is realized primarily through pressures placed on teachers to prepare students for the writing tasks associated with standardized tests. Typical formulas include ACE (Answer + Cite evidence + Explain) and RAGE (Restate + Answer + Give example + Explain). Critical educators assert that teaching writing as a formula ultimately disempowers students. Because formulaic writing holds the control over what, where, when, and how students write, students easily lose agency over the formation of their own ideas.

59   **Freewriting** is a prewriting technique in which a student writes continuously for a set period of time without regard to spelling, grammar, or topic. It produces raw, often unusable, material, but it helps writers overcome blocks of apathy and self-criticism. Freewriting can be used to generate ideas and clear out distracting thoughts. The technique is used mainly by prose writers and writing teachers.

60   **Function**, in writing instruction, describes the purpose of the written communication. Writing that is driven by function over form focuses on the intent of the writing and the needs and expectations of the audience. This emphasis results in openness to a wide variety of forms and modes, and supports a design-oriented approach to writing.

61   A **functionalist** subscribes to a theory of the mind called *functionalism*, which sees mental states (such as beliefs, desires, etc.) as constituted solely by their functional role. That is, they have causal relations with other mental states, numerous sensory inputs, and behavioral outputs. Functionalism developed largely as an alternative to the *identity theory of mind* and *behaviorism*.

62   In education, **gatekeepers** are mechanisms of inclusion and exclusion. Gatekeepers control access to challenging curriculum through criteria related to admissions and ability grouping, and may include standardized assessments. Gatekeepers tend to privilege existing relations of power and thus perpetuate inequities.

63   **Gender theory/Queer theory: Gender theory,** developed in the academy during the 1970s and 1980s, proposes looking at masculinity and femininity as sets of mutually created characteristics shaping the lives of men and women. It challenged ideas of masculinity and femininity and of men and women as operating according to fixed biological determinants. The term "gender" appeared in the early 20th century in anthropology (see

the work of Margaret Mead), and in philosophy/literature (see the work of Simone de Beauvoir). **Queer theory** is a field of post-structuralist critical theory that emerged in the early 1990s out of the field of queer studies and women's studies. Queer theory focuses on mismatches between and among sex, gender, and desire.

64   **Great Books** is associated with the *Great Books Foundation*, which is a nonprofit educational organization which publishes collections of classic and modern literature as part of reading and discussion programs for children and adults. Established in 1947 by a group of prominent citizens led by University of Chicago Chancellor Robert Maynard Hutchins and philosopher/ educator Mortimer Adler, the Great Books Foundation began as a grassroots movement to promote liberal education for the general public. Great Books discussions use a distinctive method called *shared inquiry* in which the leader starts with an open-ended question about the meaning of the selection and then asks follow-up questions to help participants develop their ideas. However, for most of its history, and particularly since the inception of Junior Great Books in 1960, the foundation has rejected Adler's narrow view of "great books" as almost entirely the product of Western males.

65   **Hidden curriculum** is the *unintended curriculum* which is not planned but may change the behavior, attitudes, or learning outcomes of students. The hidden curriculum can affect learning through, for example, the physical condition of the classroom or school, the mood of the teacher or students, the teacher-learner interaction, and peer influence. The concept of the hidden curriculum also refers to the unspoken or implicit values, behaviors, and norms that exist in an educational setting, i.e., information and skills that everyone knows but no one is taught. This includes assumed rules, adult or student expectations, and idioms.

66   **High-stakes standardized assessments**. When standardized test results are used to make important decisions about students, teachers, administrators, schools, and school districts, they are said to be high-stakes. Since the federal *No Child Left Behind* and *Race to the Top* legislative initiatives, the "high-stakes," or consequences of standardizing, include retention/promotion/ scholarship/remediation for students, transfer/dismissal/loss of licensure for teachers and administrators, and designations such "at risk" or "need of improvement" for schools and school districts. Proponents of high-stakes testing believe that it serves as an objective measure of accountability; critics contend that high-stakes testing 1) narrows the curriculum as teachers focus primarily on content which appears on the test; 2) draws time away from instruction as teachers engage in test preparation; and 3) ultimately perpetuates societal inequities by not factoring in conditions such as poverty.

67   **Horizontal alignment** is a critical part of a coherent curriculum. An effective written curriculum has horizontal coherence and vertical

coherence. When a curriculum is aligned horizontally, the content and skills being taught are mirrored across a grade level for a specific subject. In English language arts, for example, horizontal alignment would occur if all grade 9 students had access to the same content and skills. Ideally, horizontal alignment would include the same set of assessments and evaluations.

68   In the sociology of education, **identity construction** is the process of development involving life experiences, including institutional structures, and how these experiences define and categorize human perceptions (including self-perceptions) and interactions with others. Identity construction is ongoing and mutually influential with cultural factors such as language.

69   **Implicit curriculum** (see also informal curriculum) refers to lessons that are not explicitly taught. Unintended learning is pervasive in the transaction of the formal curriculum. The informal curriculum is sometimes linked to a school's co-curricular activities in which students learn a range of skills through the act of participation.

70   **Informal curriculum** (see also implicit curriculum) refers to lessons that are not explicitly taught. Unintended learning is pervasive in the transaction of the formal curriculum. The informal curriculum is sometimes linked to a school's co-curricular activities in which students learn a range of skills through the act of participation.

71   **Institutional mechanisms** are the forces within social structures, such as schools and public agencies, that influence access to wealth and cultural capital. For example, discipline policies that have differential effects on students of different races are institutional mechanisms that affect access to educational opportunities and credentials, thus altering the life chances of youth.

72   An **instrumental** approach to education is primarily focused on the development of skills, dispositions, and abilities related to job and career readiness. Instrumental perspectives of the purpose of education is prevalent in P12 institutions, as well as in post-secondary settings.

73   **Interdisciplinarity** involves the combining of two or more academic disciplines into one activity (e.g., a research project). It draws knowledge from several fields such as sociology, anthropology, psychology, economics, etc. Interdisciplinarity seeks to create something new by thinking across boundaries. Since a "discipline" is a branch of study, interdisciplinarity is the employment of *multiple disciplines* in the examination of a specific topic.

74   **International Baccalaureate** (IB), founded in 1968, is a non-profit educational foundation offering four highly respected programs of international education designed to develop intellectual, personal, emotional, and social skills needed to live and work in an increasingly globalized world. The IB diploma program is a two-year educational program aimed at 16 to 18-year-old students. The program provides an internationally accepted

qualification for entry into higher education and is recognized by many universities worldwide.

75   **Literacy** conventionally refers to skills associated with reading and writing. Contemporary understandings of literacy extend to include discourses related to various categories of knowledge and disciplines, as well as multimodal expressions and interpretations of a wide range of texts.

76   The **literary canon**, also referred to as the "Western canon," is the body of literature that scholars generally accept as the most important and influential in shaping Western culture. There has been an ongoing debate over the nature and status of the canon since at least the 1960s, much of which is rooted in critical theory, feminism, critical race theory, and Marxism. Postmodern studies have argued that the canon is biased because the focus of academic studies of Western culture has been on works produced by Western males. Multiculturalists want to include more works by women and minorities.

77   **Literature** is often defined in accordance with elite conceptions of discourse and conventional modes of writing. As such, texts traditionally categorized as literature tend to reinforce power relations associated with dominant representations of cultural capital and marginalize authors from historically underrepresented groups.

78   **Marxist theory** is best understood as answers to 19th-century German socialist Karl Marx's pointed questions about the nature and development of capitalism; specifically, how do the ways in which people earn their living affect their bodies, minds, and ways of living? According to Marxian theory, class conflict arises in capitalist societies due to contradictions between the material interests of the oppressed proletariat (wage laborers) and those of the bourgeoisie (the ruling class).

79   A **meritocracy** is a system in which the talented are chosen and moved ahead on the basis of their achievement rather than on class privilege or wealth. American culture nurtures many myths about the moral value of hard work (the phrase "by the bootstraps" is still widely used to describe Americans who have found success through a combination of dogged work and stubborn will), despite social and institutional structures that contribute to the perpetuation of inequities.

80   **Multicultural education** refers to instructional practices that embrace and celebrate cultural differences. A multicultural curricular approach emphasizes the experiences and contributions of all groups, intending to cultivate and foster full participation in a pluralistic society.

81   **Multimodal composition** involves the creation of texts that use a variety of vehicles to communicate messages and meanings. In addition to (and sometimes instead of) words and letters, multimodal composition can employ images such as photographs, paintings, and sketches, as well as audio and video clips. Multimodal composition intentionally opens possibilities for innovative formats to share thoughts and feelings.

82   **New Criticism** is a literary theory that emphasizes texts as prescribed, closed, carriers of predetermined meaning. According to this theory, texts have within them everything necessary for constructing meaning, so sociological, historical, and philosophical background information is not necessary. From the perspective of New Criticism, close reading, often multiple times to reveal layers of meaning embedded in literary elements, is considered to be the best strategy for discovering meaning in a text.

83   **New Literacy Studies** is a movement that shifts the focus of literacy development from a print-centric, individual cognitive endeavor to a multimodal, social orientation. Fluency with letters and words matters, but is augmented by audio and visual components. Further, the social nature of language and literacy is emphasized, as are various contexts in which discourses are created and used.

84   The **null curriculum** refers to content, skills, and dispositions that are neither taught by teachers nor experienced by learners in schools.

85   According to the National Council of Teachers of English, **opportunity-to-learn standards** provide a framework that makes it possible for all students to have equitable access to high-quality education. Rather than focusing primarily on outcomes in skills or content knowledge, opportunity-to-learn standards emphasize equity of opportunity to develop fully all-human capacities.

86   Defined in this terminology by Berliner, **out-of-school-factors (OSF)** are circumstances related to poverty that hinder students' ability to achieve academic success. Factors include "(1) low birth-weight and non-genetic prenatal influences on children; (2) inadequate medical, dental, and vision care, often a result of inadequate or no medical insurance; (3) food insecurity; (4) environmental pollutants; (5) family relations and family stress; and (6) neighborhood characteristics."

87   **Outcomes–based standards**, as the term implies, reflect a product-oriented framework for learning and teaching. Curriculum and instruction are developed and implemented with clear, evidence-based goals in mind, and assessments are often closely associated with observable results.

88   **Pedagogy** refers to the art, science, craft, theory, and practice of teaching. The term encompasses a range of ideologies and activities, from theories about teaching and learning, to lesson planning and assessment. It is important to keep in mind that the theoretical basis from which teachers function – that is, the beliefs and assumptions that undergird their action – influence the ways in which strategies are enacted by teachers and experienced by learners.

89   **Prescriptive standards** provide explicit descriptions of what learners should know and be able to do. Generally associated with particular age and grade level competencies, prescriptive standards describe with exact specifications the content knowledge and skills learners should demonstrate.

90   In writing instruction, a **process** approach is often differentiated from a product-oriented approach. Writing instruction focusing on process emphasizes writing as thinking, and as a means of discovery. Assessment, from a process perspective, values practices associated with writing as well as the results.

91   **Process standards** involve the development of skills related to the act of learning. Process standards include activities such as metacognition and self-reflectivity, as well as analysis, goal-setting, and inquiry. Not associated with any particular discipline, process skills pertain to any content area, and facilitate interdisciplinary applications. Process standards are thus distinct from content standards and outcomes-based standards.

92   In English classrooms, texts are **produced** when students use language to communicate. Production can be traditional, as in written texts, or involve the design and development of multimodal, innovative texts.

93   In writing instruction, the **product** is the written result ultimately submitted by students. The product is generally used to assess progress in writing.

94   A **product-oriented** approach to writing instruction focuses on the submitted result of the lesson, which is the primary source used to evaluate achievement in writing. This contrasts with a process-oriented approach to writing instruction, which emphasizes the practice of writing as a mode of thinking and communicating.

95   According to Edward Said, a **public intellectual** is responsible for enacting roles in three domains. These are 1) disciplinary knowledge, which includes adding to the field and ensuring that expertise is imparted to future generations; 2) the social context, which encompasses social and political issues with global and local implications; and 3) the infinite body of knowledge that exists beyond the boundaries of his/her disciplinary area – a domain which requires relentless curiosity and humility.

96   Social capital is produced and **re-produced** through personal and institutional practices. For example, schools privilege certain forms of academic literacy, in part because these forms of literacy are produced in the upper realms of society. By valuing these forms of literacy, schools – as social institutions – re-produce existing relations of power. Students who are fluent with academic literacy have greater opportunity to succeed in school, and students whose literacy experiences do not correspond to academic literacy are at a disadvantage. Differential achievement and resulting educational opportunities thus re-produce social capital.

97   **Reader Response Criticism** is a literary theory that emphasizes the importance of readers as essential to the process of making meaning from texts. In English classrooms, reader response is a student-centered theory of literature, since the experiences of learners are essential to the meanings that are derived from and through texts.

98   The **received curriculum** refers to how learners experience the written and delivered curriculum. Instructional content and practices are subject to interpretation at every phase of development and implementation, so the received curriculum, as experienced and described by learners, may differ significantly from the plan presented in the written curriculum.

99   In English classrooms, **receptive skills** are abilities related to the consumption of language and texts. Traditionally, receptive skills have been described as listening and reading; however, as the field grows and understandings of literacies expand, receptive skills related to multimodal texts and visual literacies have become recognized as relevant in making meaning.

100   **Reflective resistance** is an approach that involves educators engaging in subversive activities against policies or mandates that are harmful to learners. Like critical compliance, such actions are ethical, painstakingly considered, and grounded in professional principles. Critical compliance and reflective resistance provide avenues for educators to act as public intellectuals, modeling a democratic process that values dissent *and* builds consent through communication.

101   When education is perceived as an instrumental aspect of society, **return on investment** is defined as the idea that the resources employed toward schooling and earning credentials should be compensated by increased income or capital gain.

102   The Greek root meaning of **schema** is shape or plan. This duality provides a useful way of understanding the term schema, which represents both a framework for comprehension and content of background knowledge. If previous experience is symbolized by a file cabinet, for example, schema would be both the cabinet, itself, which provides a system for organization, and the materials within the cabinet, which exemplify prior knowledge.

103   A **scripted lesson** is an instructional plan that provides prescriptive directions for teachers to follow and standardized sets of materials, including assessments. Scripted lessons often provide guidelines for timing, as well as specific language for teachers and expected responses from students. Schools that adopt scripted lesson planning tend to do so in response to standardized accountability systems.

104   **Social class** refers to groupings in society broadly related to wealth, education, income, and career type. Each of these categories, which are interconnected and fluid, is associated with various levels of status and cultural capital. Social class divisions are socially constructed and can be fluid.

105   A **social construction** is a concept that is defined through collective understandings and activities. For example, status attributed to particular language dialects is entirely constructed by existing relations of power and privilege. Various dialects, in and of themselves, are equally effective in their ability to communicate thoughts, ideas, and information. However,

different dialects are judged differently on the basis of socially constructed beliefs about merit and superiority.

106   **Social mechanisms** are the systems that create and sustain power and privilege. Social systems are perpetuated through social institutions, such as schools, which provide access to educational opportunities and credentials. Social mechanisms are also maintained through entities that uphold criteria related to admissions. Finally, social mechanisms are connected to wealth and income, which influence access to structures that support possibilities for social mobility.

107   A **socioculturally focused theory of literature** grounds engagement with texts in social and cultural experiences and understandings. This tends to occur in two milieus. First, the readers seek to understand the society and culture in which the text was constructed. Second, the text is interpreted in relation to the society and culture of the reader. Both milieus are significant, and intersect dialogically. A sociocultural focus emphasizes meaning-making through and with literature as a relational, cultural endeavor.

108   A **spiral curriculum** is an intentionally recursive approach to the development of content knowledge and skills. In a spiral curriculum, skills are introduced and then revisited with increased complexity as the curriculum progresses. For example, learners might be expected to craft a thesis statement in elementary school, and to accomplish the same objective in high school; however, the expectations regarding vocabulary and conceptual depth would be greater for secondary students. Similarly, developing writers can be introduced to punctuation conventions that become increasingly sophisticated as writers mature.

109   **Stakeholders** are those who are invested in an endeavor, project, or process. Stakeholders are generally perceived to have both interest in and rights regarding how decisions are made and how resources are used.

110   **Standardized assessments** generally refer to two characteristics of the test: content and scoring. With respect to content, a standardized assessment provides a common set of questions in a prescribed format within a specific timeframe. Scoring must occur through a uniform process that allows results to be compared. Because of their consistency, standardized assessments are often perceived to be objective; however, they have been shown to reflect biases that benefit students from historically privileged backgrounds and have deleterious effects for students whose backgrounds do not correspond to academic cultural norms.

111   Literacy instruction based on a **student-centered theory of literature** emphasizes student experiences and prior knowledge as fundamental for their making meaning with text. This approach differs from two alternative approaches – one that centers the text as product and the other that centers the sociocultural milieus in which the text was produced and in which the text is consumed.

112   Latin for "blank slate," **tabula rasa** refers to the idea that learners enter classrooms in a pristine state, clear of predetermined thoughts or expectations. This conception allows education systems to perpetuate beliefs about equity that ignore opportunity standards and differences in cultural capital that influence student achievement. Further, the tabula rasa approach to teaching disregards funds of knowledge that students bring to classrooms.

113   Consistent with a close-reading approach to literacy development, a **text-centered theory of literature** underscores the product of the text as the essential carrier of meaning. Text is meant to be comprehended through decoding efforts, often involving multiple readings.

114   In a broad sense, a **text** is an artifact through which meaning is shared. A text can refer to a multimodal product that is durable or ephemeral, and can be interpreted as part of an engaged process or as a product that serves as a static carrier of meaning.

115   The **transmission model**, or banking model, of education is attributed to educational scholar and activist Paolo Freire. In this conception of education, learners are perceived as "blank slates" or "empty vessels" and the role of teachers is to transmit existing knowledge into students. This model of education presents education as a passive experience of replicating authoritative knowledge.

116   From a traditional perspective, disciplines are branches of knowledge. These branches might interconnect at the surface level, but the connections are neither deep nor structural. To improve this model, disciplines might serve not as branches, but as interconnected roots from which students can grow new knowledge. If disciplines are envisioned as roots, bonds among disciplines grow naturally and are mutually strengthening. Rather than interdisciplinary literacy, this is referred to as "**undisciplined English.**" Undisciplined English is rooted in disciplinary knowledge, but intentionally cultivates critical dispositions toward learning through projects and assessments that are authentic and relevant to the lives of learners.

117   **Value standards** refer to attitudes and behaviors related to processes of learning. Examples of such dispositions involve characteristics such as motivation, persistence, curiosity, and collaboration.

118   In a coherent curriculum, **vertical alignment** describes a progression, from grade level to grade level, in which learners develop content knowledge and skills that will enable them to successfully engage with the expectations at the next level. Vertical alignment further denotes a lack of unnecessary repetition, so that learner development is efficient and logically organized.

119   **Written curriculum** (see also explicit curriculum or formal curriculum) is that which is published as part of formal instruction in a school. It may refer to a curriculum *document*, texts, and other supportive materials that are *overtly chosen* to support the intentional instructional agenda of a school.

Works Cited

Bartholomae, David. "Inventing the University." In *Composition in Four Keys: Inquiring into the Field*. (Mark Wiley, Barbara Gleason, and Louise Weatherbee Phelps, Editors). London, UK and Toronto, Canada: Mayfield Publishing Company, pp. 460–479, 1996.

Berliner, David C. *Poverty and Potential: Out-of-School Factors and School Success*. Boulder, CO and Tempe, AZ: Education and the Public Interest Center & Education Policy Research Unit, 2009. http://nepc.colorado.edu/publication/poverty-and-potential.

Bourdieu, Pierre. "The Forms of Capital." In *Handbook of Theory and Research for the Sociology of Education*John Richardson (Editor). New York, NY: Greenwood, pp. 241–258, 1986.

Cuban, Larry. *Thinking about 'Corporate Reform': Reflections on Language*. Larry Cuban on School Reform and Classroom Practice. May 14, 2012. https://larrycuban.wordpress.com/2012/05/13/thinking-about-corporate-reform-reflections-on-language/.

Decuir, Jessica and Adrienne Dixson. "So When It Comes Out, They Aren't That Surprised That It Is There": Using Critical Race Theory as a Tool of Analysis of Race and Racism in Education." *Educational Researcher*, 33, pp. 26–31, 2004.

Ladson-Billings, Gloria. "Culturally Relevant Teaching: The Key to Making Multicultural Education Work." In *Research and Multicultural Education* (Carl A. Grant, Editor). London, UK: Falmer Press, pp. 106–121, 1992.

NCTE Executive Committee. *Opportunity-to-Learn Standards, Statement of Principles*. National Council of Teachers of English, 1996. www2.ncte.org/statement/opptolearnstandards/.

Said, Edward. *Representations of the Intellectual*. New York, NY: Vintage Books, 1994.

Tuck, Eve K. and Wayne Yang. "Decolonization is Not a Metaphor." *Decolonization: Indigeneity, Education, & Society*, vol. 1, no 1, pp. 1–40, 2012.

INDEX